African American History

TABLE OF CONTENTS

CHAPTER OVERVIEW

1: AFRICAN ORIGINS – HISTORY AND CULTURE

1.1: Introduction

African Origins—History and Culture

Module Introduction

Module 1 explores the rich histories and diverse cultures of West African peoples from antiquity to the early nineteenth-century. In the process, it addresses such questions as:

- Who were the African people who migrated to the Americas, voluntarily and involuntarily?
- What regions of Africa did they come from?
- What were their African societies like?
- What were their cultural patterns and everyday lives like before they came? [3]

It is important to learn about the history and heritage of African Americans that extends back into antiquity because throughout slavery and afterwards, people of European descent advanced what anthropologist Melville J. Herskovits called the "Myths of the Negro Past. (Drake 1990:1–14)." These myths were advanced particularly and primarily about African Americans as rationales to justify slavery, and later discrimination and segregation. [3] They advanced these myths, which portrayed Africa as a primitive and backward place, a 'Dark Continent,' to justify slavery and create ideas of race and racial inferiority. Module 1 reveals how erroneous these myths were. It demonstrates how West Africa, the area that became the center of the Atlantic slave trade, nurtured and grew technologically and intellectually advanced, and economically powerful, civilizations well before the arrival of European slave traders. [1]

Learning Outcomes

This module addresses the following Course Learning Outcomes listed in the Syllabus for this course:

- To provide students with a general understanding of the history of African Americans within the context of American History.
- To motivate students to become interested and active in African American history by comparing current events with historical information.[1]

Additional learning outcomes associated with this module are:

- The student will be able to discuss the origins, evolution, and spread of racial slavery.
- The student will be able to describe the creation of a distinct African-American culture and how that culture became part of the broader American culture. [1]

Module Objectives

Upon completion of this module, the student will be able to:

- Discuss the distinguishing features of West African civilizations.
- Refute ideas of Africa as a "Dark Continent." [1]

Readings and Resources

Learning Unit: West African Histories and Cultures (see below) [1]

CC licensed content, Original

- **Authored by**: Florida State College at Jacksonville. **License**: *CC BY: Attribution*

Public domain content

- Park Ethnography Program. **Provided by**: National Park Service. **Located at**: https://www.nps.gov/ethnography/aah/aaheritage/histContextsA.htm. **Project**: African American Heritage and Ethnography. **License**: *Public Domain: No Known Copyright*

1.2: Africans before Captivity

West African Histories and Cultures

Africans before Captivity

Most Africans who came to North America were from West Africa and West Central Africa. (See Figure 1-1) Western Africa begins where the Sahara Desert ends. A short erratic, rainy season supports the sparse cover of vegetation that defines the steppe like Sahel. The Sahel serves as a transition to the Sudan and classic savanna where a longer rainy season supports baobab and acacia trees sprinkled across an open vegetative landscape dominated by bushes, grasses and other herbaceous growth. Next comes another narrow transitional zone, where the savanna and forest intermingle, before the rain forest is reached. Finally, there is the coast, fringed with mangrove swamps and pounded by heavy surf (Newman 1995:104). The Sahara is likened to a sea lying north of West Africa and the Sahel to its shore. The desert and the Sahel form geographical barriers to sub-Saharan West Africa that, like of the Atlantic Ocean, contributed to the comparative isolation of the region from civilizations in Europe and the Middle East until the 15th century.

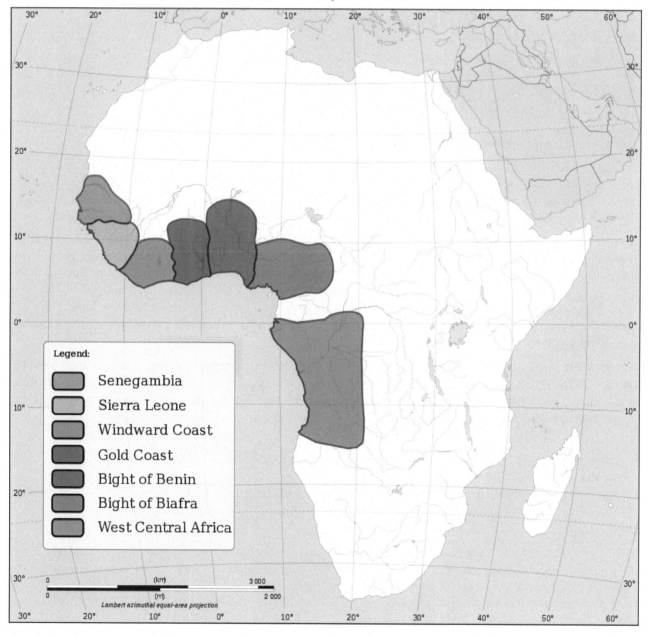

Legend:
- Senegambia
- Sierra Leone
- Windward Coast
- Gold Coast
- Bight of Benin
- Bight of Biafra
- West Central Africa

Figure 1-1 : African Slave regions by Grin20 is licensed under CC BY-SA 2.5 . Map depicting major slave trading regions of Africa.

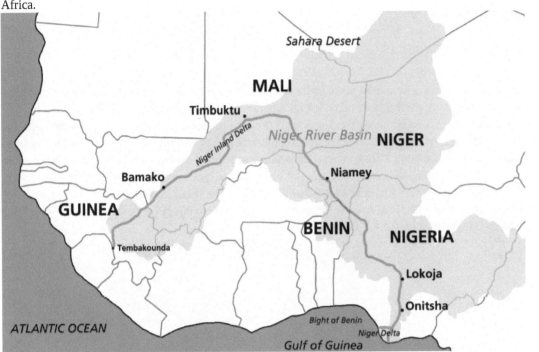

Figure 1-2 : Niger river map , a derivative of Niger river map by Wizardist is licensed under CC BY-SA 3.0 . Map of the Niger River Basin and its inland delta.

Knowledge of sub-Saharan West Africa is limited for the period before 800 A.D., after which the rise of Islam made Arabic records available, according to Phillip Curtin (1990:32). Evidence from Dar-Tchitt, an archeological site in the area of Ancient Ghana, suggests agricultural expansion and intensification gave rise to walled villages of 500–1000 inhabitants as early as 900–800 B.C. By 700 B.C. the settlement patterns changed to smaller, somewhat more numerous and unwalled villages.

Jenne-Jeno, a second archeological site, was first settled around 250 B.C. Located around the inland delta of the Niger river, Jenne-Jeno probably started out as a place where local farmers, herders, and fisher folk brought produce to exchange with one another. (See Figure 1-2) Over time the location became an interregional trade center. It might have been the first one in the region, but if so others soon followed and several of these became sites for a series of kingdoms and empires in the Sahel and Sudan. Eventually the region was densely populated by people who had a social organization based on kinship ties and political forms that are properly called states, and cities based on Saharan trade, at least as far south as modern day Djenne, which is between Timbuktu and Bamako in southern Mali.

What we know comes from Berber travelers, who made their first visits to the region in the 8th century (Curtin 1990:45; Newman 1995:109–110). Oral sources included African poems, praise songs, and accounts of past events usually passed on through official oral historians such as Griots, who recite the histories from Ancient Mali and Songhai often while playing stringed instruments unique to West Africa such as the Kora and Ngoni. [3]

CC licensed content, Shared previously

1.3: Medieval West Africa

Medieval West Africa

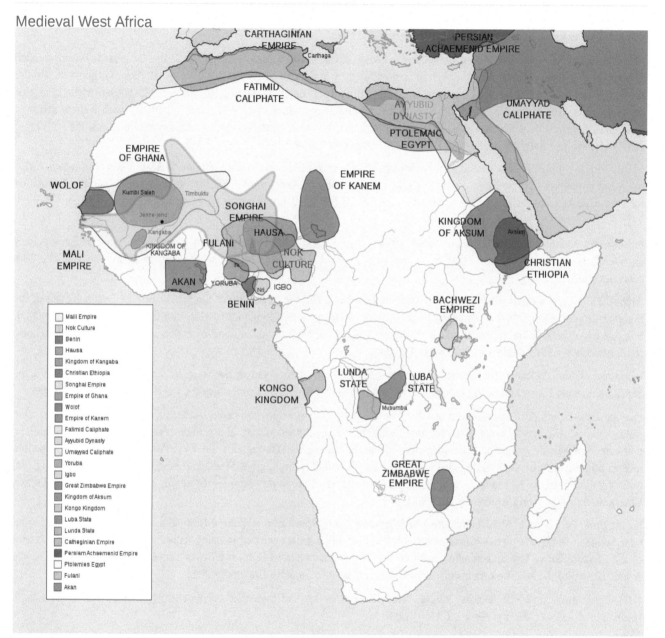

Figure 1-3 : African-civilizations-map-pre-colonial by Jeff Israel is licensed under CC BY-SA 3.0 . Map depicting major slave trading regions of Africa.

When the Portuguese first explored the West African coastline, the cultures of African societies were highly evolved and had been so for centuries. In the millennium preceding Portuguese exploration, three large centers of medieval African civilization developed sequentially along the west coast of sub-Saharan Africa. (See Figure 1-3)

The first polity that is known to have gained prominence was Ancient Ghana. Between 500 AD–1250 AD, Ancient Ghana flourished in the southern Sahel north of the middle Niger and middle Senegal Rivers. Ancient Ghana had a civil service, strong monarchy based on a matrilineal system of inheritance, a cabinet, an army, an effective justice system and a regular source of income from trade as well as tribute from vassal kings (Boahen 1966:4–9).

As Ghana declined over the next 200 years, the ancient Mali Empire arose in the same area but descended territorially further along the Niger River. Mali encompassed a huge area stretching from the Lower Senegal and Upper Niger rivers eastward to

the Niger bend and northward to the Sahel.

Its great size made Mali an even more diverse state than Ghana. The majority of the people lived in small villages and cultivated rice or sorghums and millets, while some communities specialized in herding and fishing. Trade flourished in the towns, which housed a wide array of craftspeople, along with a growing number of Islamic teachers and holy men. The main commercial centers were its capitals Niani, Timbuktu, and Gao.

Mansa Musa is the most remembered of the kings of Mali. During Musa's reign 1307–1337, Mali's boundaries were extended to their farthest limits. There were fourteen provinces ruled by governors or *emirs* who were usually famous generals. Berber provinces were governed by their own *sheiks* . They all paid tribute to Musa in gold, horses and clothes. Musa instituted national honors for his provincial administrators to encourage devoted service. He ruled impartially with a great sense of justice. To help in this work he had judges, scribes and civil servants. Musa established diplomatic relationships with other African states, especially Morocco, with whom he exchanged ambassadors.

Mansa Musa is probably best known as the ruler who firmly established the Islamic religion in Mali along with peace, order, trade and commerce. Mansa Musa started the practice of sending students to Morocco for studies and he laid the foundation for what later became the city of Timbuktu, the commercial and educational center of the western Sudan (Boahen 1966:17–22).

Present day Mande people trace their ancestry back to the great 13th century. Learn more about what archeology has uncovered in Jeno-Jenne about the past of the Mande people , Africans who helped settle America during the 17th and 18th centuries (Hall 1992:45).

Around 1375, Gao, a small tributary state of Mali, broke away under the leadership of Sunni Ali and thus began the rise of the Songhai Empire. Over the next 28 years, Sunni Ali converted the small kingdom of Gao into the huge empire of Songhai. Songhai encompassed the geographic area of ancient Ghana and Mali combined and extended into the region of the Hausa states of ancient and contemporary northwest Nigeria.

Mandinka, Wolof, Bamana, (also called Bambara) peoples, and others lived in the western reaches of the Songhai in the Senegambia area. Hausa and Fulani people lived in the region that is now northwest Nigeria. All of these cultures still exist.

Islamic scholars and African oral traditions document that all of these states had centralized governments, long distance trade routes, and educational systems. Between the 13th and 17th centuries Mande and Mande-related warriors established the dominance of Mande culture in the Senegambia geographical region. Throughout the West African savanna where people migrated in advance of the Mande warriors, people spoke mutually intelligible Mandekan languages, and had a strong oral history tradition. In the 18th century people of the Mande culture were highly represented among those enslaved in the French Louisiana colony in North America (Hall 1992).

By the time, Portugal and Spain embarked on exploration and conquest of the Western Hemisphere, Mohammed Askia I ruled over Songhai. Askia completed Mansa Musa's project to create a great center of learning, culminating with the establishment of the Sankore University in Timbuktu. Sankore teachers and students were from all over sub-Saharan Africa and from the Arabic nations to the east. Leo Africanus, an eyewitness described Sankore University thus:

"[H]ere are great stores of doctors, judges, priests and other learned men that are bountifully maintained at the King's (Muhammad Askia) costs and charges ([1600] 1896)."

Leo Africanus was born, El Hasan ben Muhammed el-Wazzan-ez-Zayyati in the city of Granada in 1485, but was expelled along with his parents and thousands of other Muslims by Ferdinand and Isabella in 1492. Settling in Morocco, he studied in Fez and as a teenager accompanied his uncle on diplomatic missions throughout North Africa. During these travels, he visited Timbuktu.

As a young man he was captured by pirates and presented as an exceptionally learned slave to the great Renaissance pope, Leo X. Leo who freed him, baptized him under the name "Johannis Leo de Medici," and commissioned him to write in Italian a detailed survey of Africa. His accounts provided most of what Europeans knew about the continent for the next several centuries.

CC licensed content, Shared previously

- African-civilizations-map-pre-colonial. **Authored by**: Jeff Israel. **Located at**: commons.wikimedia.org/wiki/File:African-civilizations-map-pre-colonial.svg. **License**: *CC BY-SA: Attribution-ShareAlike*

Public domain content

- Park Ethnography Program. **Provided by:** National Park Service. **Located at:** https://www.nps.gov/ethnography/aah/aaheritage/histContextsA.htm. **Project:** African American Heritage and Ethnography. **License:** *Public Domain: No Known Copyright*

1.4: West Africa, 1300 – 1800AD

West Africa, 1300 — 1800AD

From the 14th through the 18th century, three smaller political states emerged in the forests along the coast of Africa below the Songhai Empire. The uppermost groups of states were the Gonja or Volta Kingdoms, located around the Volta River and the confluence of the Niger, on what was called the Windward Coast, now Sierra Leone and Liberia. Most of the people in the upper region of the Windward Coast belonged to a common language group, called Gur by linguists. They also held common religious beliefs and a common system of land ownership. They lived in decentralized societies where political power resided in associations of men and women.

Below the Volta lay the Asante Empire in the southeastern geographical area of the contemporary nations of Cote d'Ivoire, Togo and modern Ghana. By the 15th century the Akan peoples, who included the Baule, and Twi-speaking Asante, reached dominance in the central region. Akan culture had a highly evolved political system. One hundred years or more before the rise of democracy in North America, the Asante governed themselves through a constitution and assembly. Commercially the Asante-dominated region straddled the African trade routes that carried ivory, gold and grain. As a result, Europeans called various parts of the region the Ivory Coast, Grain Coast and Gold Coast. The transatlantic slave trade was fed by the emergence of these Volta Kingdoms and the Asante Empire. During the 17th and early 18th centuries African people called from these regions were predominately among those enslaved in the British North American mainland colonies (Boahen 1966).

Just below the Gold Coast lay the Bights of Benin and Biafra. Oral history and findings in archeological excavation attest that Yoruba people have been the dominate group on the west bank of the Niger River as far as their historical memory extends and even further into the past. The 12th century found the Yoruba people beginning to coalesce into a number of territorial city-states of which Ife, Oyo, and Benin dominated. Old loyalties to the clan or lineage were subordinated to allegiance to a king or oni. The Oni was chosen on a rotating basis by the clans. Below him was an elected state hierarchy that depended on broad support from the community. The people were subsistence farmers, artisans, and long distance traders in cloth, kola nuts, palm oil, and copper. Trade and the acquisition of horses were factors in the emergence of Oyo as the dominant political power among the Yoruba states by late 14th and early 15th century (Boahen 1966).

Dahomey, or Benin, created by the Fon ruling dynasty, came to dominance in the 17th century and was a contemporary of the Asante Empire. As early as the 17th century the Oyo kingdom had an unwritten constitution with a system of political checks and balances. Dahomey, located in Southern Nigeria, east of Yorubaland and west of the Niger River also claimed to have obtained kingship from the Yoruba city of Ife. Oyo and Ife not only shared a common cultural history but also shared many other cultural characteristics, such as religious pantheons, patrilineal descent groups, urbanized settlement patterns, and a high level of artistic achievement by artisans, particularly in ivory, wood, brass and bronze sculpture.

Relatively few Yoruba and Fon people, the two principal ethnic groups in the Oyo kingdoms, were enslaved in North America. Most were carried to Santa Domingo (Haiti) and Brazil. During and after the Haitian Revolution, some of the Fon people who were enslaved in Haiti immigrated voluntarily or involuntarily to New Orleans (Hall 1992).

The Ibo people, the third principal group found around the Bight of Biafra in the southeastern part of the region, predominated among those enslaved in the Chesapeake region during the late 17th and early 18th century. Later in the 18th century Africans, whom the Europeans called the "Congos," i.e. Kongos, and "Angolas," predominated among those enslaved in Virginia and the Low Country plantations of colonial South Carolina (Curtin, 1969; Morgan 1998:63; Eltis et al 2002). [3]

Public domain content

1.5: West Central Africa, 14th – 18th Centuries

West Central Africa, 14th — 18th Centuries

In the century before Portuguese exploration of West Africa, the Kongo was another Kingdom that developed in West Central Africa. In the three hundred years from the date Ne Lukeni Kia Nzinga founded the kingdom until the Portuguese destroyed it in 1665, Kongo was an organized, stable, and politically centralized society based on a subsistence economy. The Kongo is significant in exploring the historic contexts of African American heritage because the majority of all Africans enslaved in the Southern English colonies were from West Central Africa (Curtin 1969; Eltis et al 2001).

The Bakongo (the Kongo people), today several million strong, live in modern Democratic Republic of the Congo, Congo-Brazzaville, neighboring Cabinda, and Angola. The present division of their territory into modern political entities masks the fact that the area was once united under the suzerainty of the ancient Kingdom of Kongo, one of the most important civilizations ever to emerge in Africa, according to Robert Ferris Thompson. The Kings of the Kongo ruled over an area stretching from the Kwilu-Nyari River, just north of the port of Loango, to the river Loje in northern Angola, and from the Atlantic to the inland valley of the Kwango. (See Figure 1-4)

Thompson estimates the Kongo encompassed an area roughly equaling the miles between New York City and Richmond, Virginia, in terms of coastal distance and between Baltimore and Eire, Pennsylvania, in terms of inland breadth. Birmingham comments that by 1600, after a century of overseas contact with the Portuguese, the "complex Kongo kingdom…dominated a region more than half the size of England which stretched from the Atlantic to the Kwango (1981:29)."

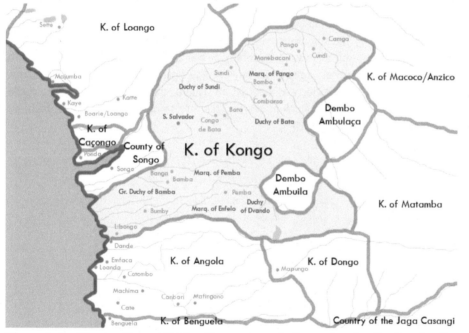

Figure 1-4 : KingdomKongo1711 by Happenstance is licensed under the Creative Commons Attribution-Share Alike 2.5 Genericlicense. The Kingdom of Kongo

The Bakongo shared a common culture with the people of eight adjoining regions, all of whom were either part of the Kongo Kingdom during the transatlantic slave trade or were part of the kingdoms formed by peoples fleeing from the advancing armies of Kongo chiefdoms. In their records slave traders called the Bakongo, as well as the people from the adjoining regions, "Congos" and "Angolas" although they may have been Mbembe, Mbanda, Nsundi, Mpangu, Mbata, Mbamba or Loango.

Ki-Kongo-speaking groups inhabited the West Central African region then known as the Loango Coast. The term Loango coast describes a historically significant area of West Central Africa extending from Cape Lopez or Cape Catherine in Gabon to Luanda in Angola. Within this region, Loango has been the name of a kingdom, a province, and a port. Once linked to the powerful Kongo Kingdom, the Loango Kingdom was dominated by the Villi, a Kongo people who migrated to the coastal

region during the 1300s. Loango became an independent state probably in the late 1300s or early 1400s. With two other Kongo-related kingdoms, Kakongo, and Ngoyo (present day Cabinda), it became one of the most important trading states north of the Congo River.

A common social structure was shared by people in the coastal kingdoms of Loango, Kakongo, Ngoyo, Vungu, and the Yombe chiefdoms; the Teke federation in the east and the Nsundi societies on either side of the Zaire River from the Matadi/Vungu area in the west to Mapumbu of Malebo pool in the east. The provincial regions, districts, and villages each had chiefs and a hierarchical system through which tribute flowed upward to the King of the Kongo and rewards flowed downward. Each regional clan or group had a profession or craft, such as weaving, basket making, potting, iron working, and so on. Tribute and trade consisted of natural resources, agricultural products, textiles, other material cultural artifacts and cowries shells (Vansima 1962; Birmingham, 1981:28–30; Bentley, 1970:75).

The "Kongos" and "Angolas" shared a " lingua franca " or trade language that allowed them to communicate. They also shared other cultural characteristics such as matrilineal social organization and a cosmology expressed in their religious beliefs and practices.

Woman-and-child figures are visual metaphors for both individual and societal fertility among Kongo Peoples and reflect their matrilineal social organization, that is, tracing their kinship through their mother's side of the family. (See Figure 1-5)

Cosmology is a body of collective representations of the world as a whole, ordered in space and time, and a human's place in it.

Fu-Kiau, the renowned Kongo scholar, was the first writer to make Kongo cosmology explicit (Fu-Kiau 1969). According to Fu Kiau Bunseki,:

"The Kongo cosmogram is the foundation of Kongo society. The circle made by the sun's movement is the first geometric picture given to human beings. We move the same way the sun moves: we wake up, are active, die, then come back. The horizon line is the kalunga line between the physical and spiritual world. It literally means 'the line of God.' When you have a circle of the Kongo cosmogram, the center is seen as the eternal flame. It is a way to come closer to the core of the community. If someone is suffering, they say 'you are outside the circle, be closer to the fire.' To stand on the cosmogram is to tie a social knot, bringing people together. Dikenga is from the verb kenga, which means 'to take care, to protect,' but also the flame or fire from inside the circle, to build and give life" (Fu-Kiau 2001).

Figure 1-5 : KongoFemaleFigure by Cliff1066 is licensed under CC BY 2.0 Before the 1920s, male and female figures carved in stone served as Kongo funerary monuments commemorating the accomplishments of the deceased. The mother and child was a common theme representing a woman who has saved her family line from extinction. Kongo mortuary figures are noted for their seated postures, expressive gestures and details of jewelry and headwear that indicate the deceased's status. The leopard claw hat is worn by male rulers and women acting as regents.

Matrilineal social organization and certain cosmological beliefs expressed in religious ceremonies and funerary practices continue to be evident in the culture of rural South Carolina and Florida African Americans who are descendants of enslaved

Africans (Brown 1987, 1988, 1989, 1994, 2000, 2001; Thompson 1984; Thompson and Cornet 1981).

European slave trade led to internal wars, enslavement of multitudes, introduction of major political upheavals, migrations, and power shifts from greater to lesser-centralized authority of Kongo and other African societies. Most notably the slave trade destroyed old lineages and kinship ties upon which the basis of social order and organization was maintained in African societies (MacGaffey 1986).

The history and culture of West Central African peoples is important to the understanding of African American people in the present because of their high representation among enslaved peoples. It has been estimated that 69 % of all African people transported in the Transatlantic Slave Trade between 1517–1700 A.D. were from West Central Africa and, between 1701–1800, people from West Central Africa comprised about 38% of the all Africans brought to the West to be enslaved (Curtin 1969). In South Carolina, by 1730, the number of Africans or "salt-water negroes," mostly from West Central Africa, and "native-born" African Americans, many descendant from West Central Africans, exceeded the white population. [3]

CHAPTER OVERVIEW

2: THE AFRICAN SLAVE TRADE AND THE ATLANTIC WORLD

2.1: Introduction

The African Slave Trade and the Atlantic World

Module Introduction

According to W.E.B. Du Bois, one of the preeminent black intellectuals and activists of the late 19th and 20th centuries, the African slave trade, which transported between 10 and 15 million Africans across the Atlantic to work as slaves in the Americas, was the most important "drama in the last thousand years of human history." The trade tore Africans away from "the dark beauty of their mother continent into the new-found Eldorado of the West. They descended into Hell." Module 2 examines the tragic history of the transatlantic slave trade that occurred between European and African traders along the west coast of Africa from the late fifteenth through the nineteenth century. It addresses why Europeans came to Africa to acquire slave labor, why powerful African kingdoms who controlled trade along the coast of Africa sold human beings to European traders in exchange for foreign commodities, how the trade generated early ideas of racial difference and systems of racism, and how the trade transformed Africa and the lives of the Africans who found themselves ensnared in a slave system sustained by cold, calculating economic rationality and human brutality.

Rather than a primitive, archaic system, the transatlantic slave trade, and the labor performed by African and African-American slaves, created the modern Western world – one characterized by a global, interconnected system of capitalist expansion. The trade regarded human beings as commodities who themselves labored to produce commodities – gold, silver, sugar, tobacco, cotton – that generated profits for plantation owners, manufacturers, and merchants. African and African-American slaves resisted enslavement at every stage and found ways to create new communities, new kinship networks, and new cultures in defiance of an inherently dehumanizing system of racial slavery that survived for more than four hundred years. [1]

Learning Outcomes

This module addresses the following Course Learning Outcomes listed in the Syllabus for this course:

- To provide students with a general understanding of the history of African Americans within the context of American History.
- To motivate students to become interested and active in African American history by comparing current events with historical information.[1]

Additional learning outcomes associated with this module are:

- The student will be able to discuss the origins, evolution, and spread of racial slavery.
- The student will be able to describe the creation of a distinct African-American culture and how that culture became part of the broader American culture. [1]

Module Objectives

Upon completion of this module, the student will be able to:

Use primary historical resources to analyze a topic relevant to Europeans, Africans, and the Transatlantic Slave Trade. [1]

Readings and Resources

- Learning Unit: Exchanging People for Trade Goods (see below) [1]
- Primary Source Documents (see below)
  - Olaudah Equiano excerpt
  - Thomas Phillips excerpt

CC licensed content, Original

- **Authored by**: Florida State College at Jacksonville. **License**: *CC BY: Attribution*

2.2: The Transatlantic Slave Trade

Exchanging People for Trade Goods

Introduction

Figure 2-1: Ottoman Empire by André Koehne is in the Public Domain . Map of the Ottoman Empire's geographical reach in the Mediterranean world from 1481 to 1683.

Europeans made the first steps toward an Atlantic slave trade in the 1440s when Portuguese sailors landed in West Africa in search of gold, spices, and allies against the Muslims and the Ottoman Empire who dominated Mediterranean trade. [2] (*See Figure 2-1*)

When the Portugese landed on the coasts of Africa they found societies engaged in a network of trade routes that carried a variety of goods back and forth across sub-Saharan Africa. Some of those goods included kola nuts, shea butter, salt, indigenous textiles, copper, iron and iron tools, and people for sale as slaves within West Africa. The arrival of European slave traders in Africa also followed Muslim traders by some eight centuries. As early as the seventh century, Muslims from North African and other areas of the Mediterranean world established trade routes into Saharan and sub-Saharan Africa and acquired gold, pepper, ivory, dried meat and hides, and slaves, which they transported to North Africa, the Middle East and beyond (Curtin 1990:40–41, Collins and Burns, *A History of Sub-Saharan Africa* (2014), 202).

As a result of the early West African slave trade by the Portuguese, a sizeable number of Africans ended up in Portugal and Spain. By the middle of the 16th century, 10,000 black people made up 10 percent of the population of Lisbon. Some had been freed while others purchased their freedom. Some were the offspring of African and Portuguese marriages and liaisons. Seville, Spain had an African population of 6,000. Some of these Africans accompanied Spanish explorers to the North American mainland. (Curtin 1990:40–11).

All of the sub-Saharan African societies discussed in Module 1 participated in the slave trade as the enslaved or as slavers or brokers. While Europeans created the demand side for slaves, African political and economic elites did the primary work of capturing, transporting and selling Africans to European slave traders on the African coast (Thornton 2002:36). Since European traders were vastly outnumbered by West Africans who controlled trade along the coast, they first had to negotiate with powerful African chiefs who often demanded tribute and fair trading terms. Only then could European traders acquire African slaves.

The reason why Africans participated in the slave trade, given its drain on the most productive adults from Africa's populations, is complex.

The violence and war sown by the slave trade greatly disrupted African societies. One answer is that the institution of slavery already existed in African societies. Slavery in Africa, however, was different from the kind of slavery that evolved in the New World, particularly the English colonies, a topic discussed in Module 3. (Curtin 1990:40–41).

Most legal systems in Africa recognized slavery as a social condition. Slaves constituted a class of people, captives or their descendants, over whom private citizens exercised the rights of the state to make laws, punish, and control. Although these rights could be sold, in practice people of the slave class who had been settled in one location for a sufficient time came to possess a number of rights, including immunity from resale or arbitrary transfer from one owner or location (Thornton 2002:43). In Kongo in west central Africa, there was no such thing as a class of slaves but many people belonged to a transitory group of servile subjects. "These were people of foreign origin, people who had been outlawed for criminal acts, people who had lost the protection of their kinfolk, or become irredeemably indebted to others," argues one historian. "They differed from those enslaved by Europeans in that under normal conditions they were likely to be reabsorbed into society (Birmingham 1981:32)."

Many of those enslaved and brought to the New World were people who had participated in local and long-distance trade. Depending upon their resources, they were skilled agriculturists; artisans of textiles, bronze, gold, ivory sculpture, jewelry and sacred objects; craftsmen of wooden tools, furniture, and architectural elements; as well as potters and blacksmiths. Others were skilled linguists in more than one African language and often one or more European languages as well. In some cases, they had developed trade languages that facilitated inter-group communication even among African people whose language they did not know.

Even though those who were enslaved became part of one of the most heinous of historical tragedies, Africans enslaved in North American also became part of one of the greatest triumphs of human history. African people and their descendants helped to develop the modern Western world and create a new nation in the process. [3]

The Transatlantic Slave Trade

The ninth through the fifteenth centuries were times of great struggle in Europe. The European powers struggled with one another for territorial and commercial dominance. Western and Eastern Christendom struggled with one another and with Islam for religious and cultural dominance.

The struggle for religious dominance resulted in North African Berbers, Mid-Eastern Arabs and other Muslim peoples from Morocco occupying the Iberian Peninsula for 700 years from 712 A.D. to 1492 A.D. During this time, while the Iberian powers sought to free themselves of Moorish occupation, England and France embarked on the Crusades to retake the Holy Land from Muslims, whom Christians called the "infidels."

The periods of the ninth to fifteenth centuries were also times of external warfare among European powers over trade, the decline of chiefdoms, and of internal consolidation, all leading to the emergence of new European states. This era was marked by the loss of agricultural productivity, famine, disease, and epidemics. Peasants rebelled against increased demands by nobility for tribute to pay for the wars. To resolve the emerging crisis, European nations increased the scale and intensity of Old World wars for commercial dominance. These circumstances combined to deplete the wealth of European nobility and the Church (Wolf 1982:108–125). [3]

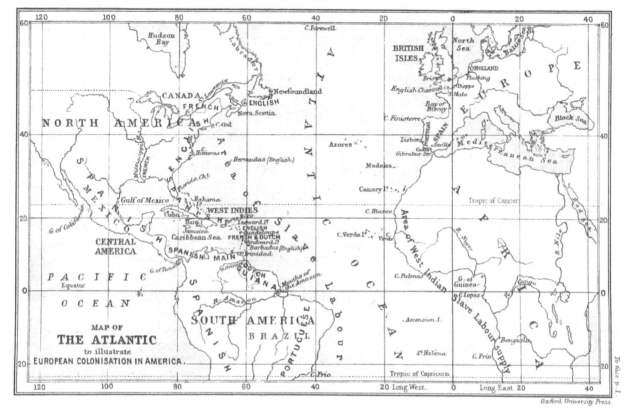

Figure 2-2: Map of the Atlantic to illustrate colonization in America (1888) by Charles P. Lucas is in the Public Domain . Map showing the Atlantic world, including the places in African where European traders acquired slaves and the regions in the Americas where Europeans used them for labor.

As the fifteenth century came to a close, Europeans embarked upon exploration of the New World and Africa in search of expanded territory, new goods, precious metals, and new markets. All of these enterprises required manpower to explore, clear land, build colonies, mine precious metals, and provide the settlers with subsistence. In the New World, Europeans first tried to meet these needs by enslaving American Indians and relying on European indentured laborers. Nevertheless, war, disease and famine among Native Americans and European settlers depleted the colonies' already limited labor supply. When both of these sources proved inadequate to meet the needs for labor, Europe turned to Africa (Wolf 1982:108–125).

The development of economies based on production of sugar, tobacco and eventually rice were contingent upon workers with particular attributes of material cultural knowledge, agricultural skills and the physical capability to acclimate to the New World environment. Africans first enslaved by the Spanish and Portuguese demonstrated that they were people who fulfilled these requirements (Wolfe 1982:108–125).

In the sixteenth century, Spanish conquistadores sailed to the Americas lured by the prospects of finding gold. They brought a few Africans as slaves with them. Early Spanish settlers soon were reporting that in mining operations the work of one African was equal to that of four to eight Indians. They promoted the idea that Africans as slaves would be essential to production of goods needed for European colonization.

Several factors combined to give impetus to the Spanish demand for an African work force. Native Americans died in large numbers from European diseases for which they had no immunity. At the same time, the Spanish clergy interceded to the Spanish Crown to protect exploitation of Indians in mining operations.

The introduction of sugarcane as a cash crop was another factor motivating the Spanish to enslave Africans. In order to turn a profit, Spanish planters needed a large, controllable work force, they turned to Africa for laborers (Reynolds 2002:14).

Once Portugal and Spain established the profitability of the African slave trade, other European nations entered the field. The English made an initial foray into the African slave trade in 1530 when William Hawkins, a merchant of Plymouth, visited the

Guinea Coast and left with a few slaves. Three decades later Hawkins' son, John, set sail in 1564 for the Guinea Coast. Supported by Queen Elizabeth I, he commanded four armed ships and a force of one hundred and seventy men. Hawkins lost many of these men in fights with "Negroes" on the Guinea coast in his attempts to secure Africans to enslave. Later through piracy he took 300 Africans from a Spanish vessel, making it profitable for him to head for the West Indies where he could sell them for money and trade them for provisions. Queen Elizabeth I rewarded him for opening the slave trade for the English by knighting him and giving him a crest that showed a Negro's head and bust with arms bound secure (Hale [1884] 1967 Vol. 3:60).

For more than a century after Columbus's voyages, only Spain and Portugal established New World settlements. England did not establish its first enduring settlement in Jamestown, Virginia, until 1607. France founded a settlement in Quebec in 1608. Henry Hudson brought Africans with him in his Dutch sponsored exploration of the river that came to bear his name. Africans also accompanied the Dutch in 1621 when they established a trading post in the area of present day Albany. [3]

Race as a Factor

European participation in African enslavement can only be partially explained by economics. At the end of the medieval period, slavery was not widespread in Europe. It was mostly isolated in the southern fringes of the Mediterranean. Iberian Christians mostly enslaved Muslims, Jews, Gypsies, and Slavs who were "white" non-Christian eastern Europeans from whose name the word "slave" derives. When the transatlantic slave trade in Africans began in 1441, Europeans placed Africans in a new category. They deemed them natural slaves — a primitive, heathen people whose dark skin confirmed their God-ordained inferiority and subservience to Christian Europeans. (Gomes 1936 in Sweet 2003:5). Europeans thus created an emergent understanding of "race" and racial difference from their participation in the transatlantic slave trade and a system of racism codified in law and policy and driven by a desire for wealth and profit. The first transnational, institutional endorsement of African slavery occurred in 1452 when the Pope granted King Alphonso V of Portugal the right to reduce all the non-Christians in West Africa to perpetual slavery (Saunders 1982:37–38 in Sweet 2003:6).

By the second half of the fifteenth century, the term "Negro" had become essentially synonymous with "slave" across the Iberian Peninsula and had literally come to represent a race of people, most often associated with black Africans and considered to be inferior (Sweet 2003:7). In the seventeenth century, Spanish colonizers created a sistema de castas, or caste system, that ranked the status, and power, of peoples based on their "purity of blood." Spanish elites born in Spain sat the top of this racial classificatory system while African slaves occupied the bottom. Skin color thus correlated with status and power. Race-based ideas of European superiority and religious beliefs in the need to Christianize "heathen" peoples contributed to a culture in which enslavement of Africans could be rationalized and justified. These explanations, however, do not answer the question of why some Africans participated in the enslavement of other Africans in the transatlantic slave trade. [3]

Figure 2- 3: Las castas mexicanas by Ignacio María Barreda is in the Public Domain .

Internal African Conflicts and Complexities

Western and African historians agree that war captives, condemned criminals, debtors, aliens, famine victims, and political dissidents were subject to enslavement within West African societies. They also agree that during the period of the transatlantic slave trade, internal wars, crop failure, drought, famine, political instability, small-scale raiding, taxation, and judicial or religious punishment produced a large number of enslaved people within African states, nations and principalities. There is general agreement among scholars that the capture and sale of Africans for enslavement was primarily carried out by the Africans themselves, especially the coastal kings and the elders, and that few Europeans ever actually marched inland and captured slaves themselves (Boahen, 1966; Birmingham 1981; Wolf 1985; Mintz 2003). African wars were the most important source of enslavement. [3] It is important to recognize, however, that there did not exist a common shared "African" identity

among African peoples during the early stages of the transatlantic slave trade along the coast of West Africa. Consequently, when traders from West African kingdoms sold men, women, and children to Europeans slave traders most would have thought they were selling outsiders, rather than fellow Africans, from their societies and kingdoms — people who spoke different languages, people who were prisoners of war or criminals, debtors and dissidents. [1]

Just as there were wars between Europeans over the right to slave catchment areas and points of disembarkation, there were increasing numbers of wars between African principalities as the slave trade progressed. Whatever the ostensible causes for these wars, they resulted in prisoners of war that supplied slave factories at Goree and Bance Islands, Elmina, Cape Coast Castle, and James Forts and at Fernando Po along the West and West Central African coast.

The fighting between African societies followed a pattern. Wars weakened the centralized African governments and undermined the authority of associations, societies, and the elders who exercised social control in societies with decentralized political forms. The winners and losers in wars both experienced the loss of people from niches in lineages, secret societies, associations, guilds and other networks that maintained social order. Conflict brought about loss of population and seriously compromised indigenous production of material goods, cash crops and subsistence crops.

Winners and losers in the African wars came to rely upon European trade goods more and more. Eventually the European monetized system replaced cowrie shells as a medium of exchange. European trade goods supplanted former African reliance on indigenous material goods, natural resources and products as the economic basis of their society. At the same time Europeans increasingly required people in exchange for trade goods. Once this stage was reached an African society had little choice but to trade human lives for European goods and guns; guns that had become necessary to wage wars for further captives in order to trade for goods upon which an African society was now dependent (Birmingham 1981: 38).

While the slave trade often enriched the West African kingdoms that controlled the trade along the coast, it had a devastating impact on the societies as a whole. African societies lost kinship networks, agricultural laborers and production. The loss of people meant the loss of indigenous artisans and craftsmen, along with the knowledge of textile production, weaving and dying, metallurgy and metalwork, carving, basket making, potting skills, architectural, and agricultural techniques upon which their societies depended. Africa's loss was the New World's gain. These were the same material cultural expertise and skills that Africans brought to the New World along with their physical labor and ability to acclimate to environmental conditions that made them indispensable in the development of the Western Hemisphere. [3]

CC licensed content, Original

- **Authored by**: Florida State College at Jacksonville. **License**: *CC BY: Attribution*

CC licensed content, Shared previously

- The American YAWP. **Provided by**: Stanford University Press. **Located at**: http://www.americanyawp.com/index.html. **License**: *CC BY-SA: Attribution-ShareAlike*

Public domain content

- Park Ethnography Program. **Provided by**: National Park Service. **Located at**: https://www.nps.gov/ethnography/aah/aaheritage/histContextsA.htm. **Project**: African American Heritage and Ethnography. **License**: *Public Domain: No Known Copyright*
- Ottoman Empire. **Authored by**: Andru00e9 Koehne. **Located at**: commons.wikimedia.org/wiki/File:Ottoman_empire.svg. **License**: *Public Domain: No Known Copyright*
- u00a0Map of the Atlantic to illustrate colonization in America (1888). **Authored by**: Charles P. Lucas. **Located at**: commons.wikimedia.org/wiki/File:Map_of_the_Atlantic_to_illustrate_euopean_colonisation_in_America_(1888).jpg. **License**: *Public Domain: No Known Copyright*
- Las castas mexicanas. **Authored by**: Ignacio Maru00eda Barreda. **Located at**: commons.wikimedia.org/wiki/File:Ignacio_Mar%C3%ADa_Barreda_-_Las_castas_mexicanas.jpg. **License**: *Public Domain: No Known Copyright*

2.3: Which Europeans Trafficked in Slaves?

Which Europeans Trafficked in Slaves?

The Portuguese dominated the first 130 years of the transatlantic African slave trade. After 1651 they fell into second position behind the British who became the primary carriers of Africans to the New World, a position they continued to maintain until the end of the trade in the early nineteenth century.

Based on data concerning 86% of all slaving vessels leaving for the New World, historians estimate that the British, including British colonials, and the Portuguese account for seven out of ten transatlantic slaving voyages and carried nearly three quarters of all people embarking from Africa destined for slavery (Eltis et al 2001).

France joined the traffic of slaves in 1624, Holland and Denmark soon followed. The Dutch wrested control of the transatlantic slave trade from the Portuguese in the 1630s, but by the 1640s they faced increasing competition from French and British traders. England fought two wars with the Dutch in the 17 th century to gain supremacy in the transatlantic slave trade.

Three special English companies were formed, including the Royal African Company, to operate in the sale of slaves. They were given the exclusive rights to trade between the Gold Coast and the British colonies in America. As the 17 th century came to a close in 1698, English merchants' protests led to the English crown extending the right to trade in slaves more generally. Colonists in New England immediately began to engage in slave trafficking. Vessels left Boston, Massachusetts and Newport, Rhode Island laden with hogsheads of rum that were exchanged for people in Africa consequently enslaved in North American and Caribbean colonies.

Beginning with the Spanish demand for slave labor, a demand that continued and expanded in the other colonies and the United States even after abolition of the trade in 1807, the Transatlantic Slave Trade brought between 9.6 to 11 million Africans to the New World (Curtin 1969; Donnan [1930]2002; Eltis et. al 2001; Hall 1992).

Greater numbers of people were sold into slavery from some regions as compared to other regions. Some European nations transported more Africans than others and some regions in the New World received more Africans from certain regions than others. The British and Portuguese account for seven out of every ten transatlantic slaving voyages and carried nearly three quarters of all people embarking from Africa destined for slavery (Eltis et al 2001). [3]

The Middle Passage

European slavers transported millions of Africans across the ocean in a terrifying journey known as the Middle Passage. Writing at the end of the eighteenth century, Olaudah Equiano, a former slave and abolitionist whose memoir helped end the British slave trade in 1807, recalled the fearsomeness of the crew, the filth and gloom of the hold, the inadequate provisions allotted for the captives, and the desperation that drove some slaves to suicide. (Equiano claimed to have been born in Igboland in modern-day Nigeria, but he may have been born in colonial South Carolina, where he collected memories of the Middle Passage from African-born slaves.) [2]

In the same time period, Alexander Falconbridge, a slave ship surgeon, described the sufferings of slaves from shipboard infections and close quarters in the hold. Dysentery, known as "the bloody flux," left captives lying in pools of excrement. Chained in small spaces in the hold, slaves could lose so much skin and flesh from chafing against metal and timber that their bones protruded. [2] Other sources detailed rapes, whippings, and diseases like smallpox and conjunctivitis aboard slave ships. [1] One historian has referred to conditions Africans endured in the Middle Passage as "probably the purest form of domination in the history of slavery as an institution." (Eltis, *The Rise of African Slavery in the Americas*, 117). [2]

"Middle" had various meanings in the Atlantic slave trade. For the captains and crews of slave ships, the Middle Passage was one leg in the maritime trade in sugar and other semi-finished American goods, manufactured European commodities, and African slaves. For the enslaved Africans, the Middle Passage was the middle leg of three distinct journeys from Africa to the Americas. First was an overland journey in Africa to a coastal slave-trading factory, often a trek of hundreds of miles. Second —and middle—was an oceanic trip lasting from one to six months in a slaver. Third was acculturation (known as "seasoning") and transportation to the American mine, plantation, or other location where new slaves were forced to labor. [2]

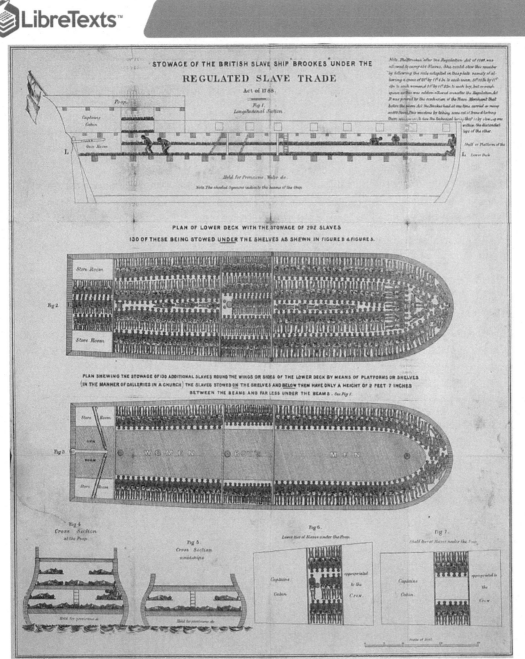

Figure 2-5: Slaveshipposter by Plymouth Chapter of the Society for Effecting the Abolition of the Slave Trade is in the Public Domain . This diagram of the British slave ship, Brookes, showing how traders stowed African slaves in order to maximize capacity. Recent estimates count between 11 and 12 million Africans forced across the Atlantic between the sixteenth and nineteenth centuries, with about 2 million deaths at sea as well as an additional several million dying in the trade's overland African leg or during seasoning. [2]

CC licensed content, Shared previously

- The American YAWP. **Provided by**: Stanford University Press. **Located at**: http://www.americanyawp.com/index.html. **License**: *CC BY-SA: Attribution-ShareAlike*

Public domain content

- Park Ethnography Program. **Provided by**: National Park Service. **Located at**: https://www.nps.gov/ethnography/aah/aaheritage/histContextsA.htm. **Project**: African American Heritage and Ethnography. **License**: *Public Domain: No Known Copyright*

2.4: Summary

Summary of Transatlantic Slave Trade

It was the labor of enslaved Africans who extracted the gold and silver from South American mines, who grew the sugar cane on Caribbean plantations, and later tobacco, rice, indigo, and cotton on North American plantations that helped power an entire system of capitalism. European capital funded slave ships who carried European goods to the coast of Africa in exchange for human beings who became slaves and by extension commodities who were bought and sold to other traders and plantation owners.

These African slaves then produced commodities grown in European colonies that traders exported to Europe for manufacturing and sale to consumers across the continent. Africans and their labor were the beating heart of this interconnected system of global trade and capitalist expansion. For instance, in one single year, 1807, Britain imported 297.9 million pounds of slave-produced sugar, 72.74 million pounds of cotton, and 16.4 million pounds of tobacco — virtually all of it produced by slaves.

In the year 1800 alone, historian Robin Blackburn estimates that about one million slaves performed labor on British controlled plantations that amounted to about "2,500,000,000 hours of toil" combined. (Blackburn, *The Making of New World Slavery* , 581, Rediker, *The Slave Ship* , 347–348). That same African slave labor in 1800 produced the equivalent of over 4 billion American dollars when adjusted for inflation in 2018.

Despite the exploitation and dehumanization they endured as slaves, Africans created new cultures and kinship ties that drew from their roots in Africa and their new experiences and contacts in the Americas. These African-American cultures would become the basis of black resistance and resilience for generations of slaves while, later, also becoming a fundamental part of the history and culture of the United States of America. [1]

CC licensed content, Original

2.5: Primary Sources

Primary Source Document: Olaudah Equiano Excerpt
Document File Link

Primary Source Document: Thomas Phillips Excerpt
Document File Link

A Brief Guide to Analyzing and Writing about Primary Sources
Document File Link

CC licensed content, Original

- A Brief Guide to Analyzing and Writing about Primary Sources. **Authored by**: Florida State College at Jacksonville. **License**: *CC BY: Attribution*

Public domain content

- The Interesting Narrative of the Life of Olaudah Equiano, Or Gustavus Vassa, The African: Written By Himselfu00a0. **Authored by**: Olaudah Equiano. **Located at**: https://archive.org/stream/theinterestingna15399gut/15399.txt. **License**: *Public Domain: No Known Copyright*
- A Journal of a Voyage Made in the Hannibal of London. **Authored by**: Thomas Phillips. **Located at**: https://books.google.com/books?id=qFJBAAAAcAAJ&printsec=frontcover&dq=Thomas+Phillips+Hannibal&hl=en&sa=X&ved=0ahUKEwiZqfHJjPnZAhVHGpAKHdRXANwQ6AEIKzAB#v=onepage&q=Thomas%20Phillips%20Hannibal&f=false. **License**: *Public Domain: No Known Copyright*

CHAPTER OVERVIEW

3: THE DEVELOPMENT INDENTURED SERVITUDE AND RACIAL SLAVERY IN THE AMERICAN COLONIES

3.1: Introduction

Servitude and Slavery in the American Colonies

Module Introduction

African and African-American slave labor helped transform European colonies in North America into important producers of coveted commodities such as tobacco, rice, indigo, and, later, cotton and sugar. Nevertheless, a colonial economy based in part on racial slavery was not inevitable in North America. Initially, colonists relied mostly on European and even African indentured servants for labor in the tobacco fields of places like Virginia and Maryland. But as these colonial societies developed in the seventeenth and eighteenth centuries, fluid labor arrangements and racial categories began to solidify into the race-based, chattel slavery that increasingly defined the economy of the Britain's North American empire. The North American mainland originally occupied a small and marginal place in that broad empire, as even the output of its most prosperous colonies paled before the tremendous wealth of Caribbean sugar islands. And yet the colonial backwaters on the North American mainland, ignored by many imperial officials, were nevertheless deeply tied into these larger Atlantic networks. A new and increasingly complex Atlantic World connected the continents of Europe, Africa, and the Americas. Patterns and systems established during the colonial era would continue to shape American society for centuries. And none, perhaps, would be as brutal and destructive as the institution of slavery. [2]

Module Three focuses on the development of racial slavery, and slave societies, in the Chesapeake colonies of Virginia and Maryland and the Low Country colonies of South Carolina and Georgia. It addresses how the growth of a tobacco economy in the Chesapeake, and the decline of indentured servitude, led to an increasing demand for and reliance on African slave labor. It also discusses how the slave societies in the tobacco based colonies of the Chesapeake differed from the rice based economies of the Low Country. Module Three also discusses how colonies like Virginia and Maryland created new laws to make racial slavery a legal category and increasingly define blackness as associated with bondage and whiteness linked with freedom. Finally, Module Three demonstrates how Africans and African-Americans in these new slave societies created enduring family bonds and kinship networks despite their legal status as chattel property. [1]

Learning Outcomes

This module addresses the following Course Learning Outcomes listed in the Syllabus for this course:

- To provide students with a general understanding of the history of African Americans within the context of American History.
- To motivate students to become interested and active in African American history by comparing current events with historical information.

Additional learning outcomes associated with this module are:

- The student will be able to discuss the origins, evolution, and spread of racial slavery.
- The student will be able to describe the creation of a distinct African-American culture and how that culture became part of the broader American culture. [1]

Module Objectives

Upon completion of this module, the student will be able to:

- Discuss the important differences between various slave societies in North America in the 17th and 18th centuries.
- Formulate an opinion as to the inevitability of racial slavery in North America. [1]

Readings and Resources

Learning Unit: Slavery in Colonial America (see below) [1]

CC licensed content, Original

- **Authored by**: Florida State College at Jacksonville. **License**: *CC BY: Attribution*

CC licensed content, Shared previously

- The American YAWP. **Provided by**: Stanford University Press. **Located at**: http://www.americanyawp.com/index.html. **License**: *CC BY-SA: Attribution-ShareAlike*

3.2: The Settling of Virginia

Slavery in Colonial America

The Settling of Virginia: The Development of a Tobacco Economy and the Arrival of the Colony's First Africans

The English failed in their first attempt to establish a colony in 1585 on Roanoke Island, one of the barrier islands off what would become North Carolina. They left little more than terrain named Virginia for the virgin Queen Elizabeth the First. Twenty-two years later, in 1607 they established a settlement they called, Jamestown, further north along the Atlantic coast at the confluence of the James River and the mouth of the Chesapeake Bay.

The Powhatan Confederacy of Native Americans populated the land surrounding the Chesapeake and from the start the natives resisted the invading English colonists. In time, Native Americans made friendly gestures to the settlers such as trading foods and introducing the English to tobacco. While the English offered the Native Americans friendship, they also brought them decimating diseases, occupied their territory, and sought to enslave or kill them. When the first Africans arrived in 1619, the colony was still under intermittent Indian attacks.

The pressing need for laborers shaped the Virginia Colony from the very beginning. More than half of the first 104 Jamestown colonists were gentlemen, scholars, artisans, and tradesmen. There were no laborers or yeomen farmers among the original settlers, people whose skills would have been invaluable in creating a foothold in the wilderness. [3]

Colliding Cultures

Little improved over the next several years. By 1616, 80 percent of all English immigrants that arrived in Jamestown had perished. England's first American colony was a catastrophe. The colony was reorganized, and in 1614 the marriage of Pocahontas, the daughter of Chief Powhatan, to John Rolfe eased relations with the Powhatan, though the colony still limped along as a starving, commercially disastrous tragedy. The colonists were unable to find any profitable commodities remained dependent upon the Indians and sporadic shipments from England for food. But then tobacco saved Jamestown.

By the time King James I described tobacco as a "noxious weed,… loathsome to the eye, hateful to the nose, harmful to the brain, and dangerous to the lungs," it had already taken Europe by storm. In 1616 John Rolfe crossed tobacco strains from Trinidad and Guiana and planted Virginia's first tobacco crop. In 1617 the colony sent its first cargo of tobacco back to England. The "noxious weed," a native of the New World, fetched a high price in Europe and the tobacco boom began in Virginia and then later spread to Maryland. Within fifteen years American colonists were exporting over 500,000 pounds of tobacco per year. Within forty, they were exporting fifteen million.

Tobacco changed everything. It saved Virginia from ruin, incentivized further colonization, and laid the groundwork for what would become the United States. With a new market open, Virginia drew not only merchants and traders, but also settlers. Colonists came in droves. They were mostly young, mostly male, and mostly indentured servants who signed contracts called indentures that bonded them to employers for a period of years in return for passage across the ocean. But even the rough terms of servitude were no match for the promise of land and potential profits that beckoned English farmers. But still there were not enough of them. Tobacco was a labor-intensive crop and ambitious planters, with seemingly limitless land before them, lacked only laborers to escalate their wealth and status. The colony's great labor vacuum inspired the creation of the "headright policy" in 1618: any person who migrated to Virginia would automatically receive 50 acres of land and any immigrant whose passage they paid would entitle them to 50 acres more.

In 1619 the Virginia Company established the House of Burgesses, a limited representative body composed of white landowners that first met in Jamestown. That same year, a Dutch slave ship sold 20 Africans to the Virginia colonists. Southern slavery was born. [2]

The First Africans in Jamestown

The Africans' arrival would not only change the course of Virginia history but the course of what would become the United States of America (See Figure 3-1). There were both men and women in this first group of Africans. Three or four days later, a second ship arrived. One additional African woman disembarked in Virginia. (Travels and Works of Captain John Smith [1910] 1967:541 as cited in Russell [1913] 1969:22 ftn.21).

The first Africans to arrive in Jamestown were welcome additions to the labor force. They were needed for the tasks of opening the wilderness, clearing land, and building settlements around the Chesapeake Bay. The first Africans, as few as they were, fulfilled a sorely needed and relatively empty labor niche in Virginia society. They and the African immigrants that followed also served another equally important purpose. Under the head-right system, they enabled the growth of a new landowning middle class located socially between the gentleman who had been granted the Virginia Company land by the Crown and the laboring class of indentured servants and slaves who worked the colony's expanding tobacco lands (See Figure 3-2).

Nine months after the arrival of the first Africans, the Census of March 1620 listed 892 English colonists living in Virginia, males outnumbering females, seven to one. Also present were 32 Africans, 15 men and 17 women, a more equal sex distribution that lent it to family formation. (Ferrar Papers 1509–1790 as cited in McCartney 2000 Vol. I: 52).

LANDING NEGROES AT JAMESTOWN
FROM DUTCH MAN-OF-WAR. 1619

Illustration titled "Landing Negroes at Jamestown from Dutch man-of-war, 1619"; signed H. Pyle in lower left-hand cornerFigure 3-1 – AfricansatJamestown1619 by Howard Pyle is in the Public Domain .

Illustration from 1670 showing African slaves curing and drying tobacco in the Virginia colony.Figure 3-2 — 1670 Virginia tobacco slaves by Unknown is in the Public Domain .

Most of the Africans who arrived in Jamestown in August 1619, remain virtually anonymous. There were three Negro men and two Negro women listed later as servants living in the Yeardley Household. Angelo, a Negro woman who disembarked from the Treasurer three or four days after the first group became a member of the Captain William Pierce household (Hotten 1874 as cited in McCartney 2000:174). Antoney, Negro and Isabell, Negro arrived in 1621 with a newborn son they immediately had baptized. Although these people and the other first African settlers are mostly lost to history, the act of baptizing their son allows us a small window into the cultural patterns and beliefs of these earliest African in America (Russell [1913] 1969:24 ftn.34).

Nearly three quarters of the Africans disembarking in the lower-Chesapeake (York and Upper James Basin) came from more southerly parts of Africa from the Bight of Biafra (Present day eastern Nigeria) and West Central Africa, then called Kongo and Angola. The inheritance practices of the Virginia gentry, especially those in York and Rappahannock districts, perpetuated the concentration of enslaved African people who had common cultural characteristics. The resulting ethnic concentration of enslaved communities originally from West Central Africa and the Bight of Biafra in these regions facilitated continuity of family and kinship networks, settlement patterns, and intergenerational transmission of African customs and languages.

Among the Africans who came, were "Antonio a Negro" in 1621 aboard the James and in 1622 the Margaret and John brought "Mary a Negro Woman (Hotten 1874 as cited in Russell [1913] 1969:24 ftn.34)." Once in Jamestown, Mary was taken to Bennett's Welcome Plantation. There she met Antonio, one of only five survivors of a recent Tidewater Indian attack that had killed 350 colonists in a single morning. Their meeting was as fortuitous as Antonio's survival of the Indian attack.

When Antonio appears in the 1625 muster of Bennett's Welcome with the anglicized name Anthony Johnson, Mary appears too as the only woman living at Bennett's plantation. Sometime after 1625, Mary and Anthony Johnson married. Once indentured servants, they were now free and owned their own land on Virginia's Eastern Shore. They soon acquired their own servants and even slaves. In 1655, Johnson won a court ruling allowing him to keep a black man named John Casar as an indentured servant despite Casar's contention that Johnson kept him as a slave (See Figure 3-3).

![Handwritten 1655 court ruling document]

Image shows a handwritten 1655 court ruling in favor of Anthony Johnson and who was accused of keeping one of his servants as a slave. The court allowed him to continue to keep a black man, named John Casar, as an indentured servant.Figure

3-3 — Court Ruling on Anthony Johnson and His Servant by Northampton County, VA Deeds, Will, etc. is in the Public Domain .

The freedom Johnson and his wife maintained, as well as their acquisition of their own land and servants and, sometimes, slaves, provides an example of the fluidity of social and race relations in Virginia's early decades. In the ensuing years and decades, as the colony's tobacco economy expanded, requiring more and more labor, legislators would pass new laws restricting black freedom and increasingly defining black people as slaves. A series of new laws passed in the late seventeenth and eighteenth century in Virginia and Maryland would slowly but surely chip away at freedom and autonomy black people like Anthony Johnson and his wife, Mary, experienced in the early and middle seventeenth before all but disappearing. [3]

The Peopling of Maryland Colony

Within twenty years following the settlement of Jamestown, Virginia, the Calvert family obtained a charter from King Charles I for land along the Chesapeake north of the Potomac River. The colony was named in honor of the king's consort, Henrietta Maria. King Charles I was deeply concerned about the presence of the Dutch in North America and decided to establish Maryland as a buffer between Virginia and the Dutch controlled New Netherlands colony in what is today the state of New York.

In the 1660s, less than 25% of Maryland's bound laborers were enslaved Africans. By 1680 the number had increased to 33% and by the early 1700s, three quarters of laborers were enslaved Africans. About 300 arrived each year between 1695 and 1708. During this time, at least half of Maryland's enslaved population lived in Calvert, Charles, Prince George's, and St. Mary's counties. The others lived in Annapolis and Baltimore.

From the beginning, the Maryland population was religiously, socially and racially diverse. Unlike the Virginians, the Maryland colonists brought Africans with them. At least two men of African descent were aboard the *Ark* and the *Dove* , ships that brought Leonard Calvert, son of George Calvert, first Lord of Baltimore, up the Chesapeake Bay in 1634. One of these first African Marylanders was Mathias de Sousa. A passenger on the *Ark* , De Sousa was of African and Portuguese descent and, like the Calvert family, he was a Catholic.

Maryland never experienced protracted Indian warfare or a "starving time" like its neighbor Virginia. Maryland was able to trade with Virginia for needed items and the Calvert family personally supported the settlers' early financial needs. However, like Virginia, Maryland suffered from a labor shortage. In order to stimulate immigration, in 1640 Maryland adopted the head-right system that Virginia had instituted earlier.

While interested in establishing a refuge for Catholics who were facing increasing persecution in Anglican England, the Calverts were also interested in creating profitable estates. To this end, they encouraged the importation of Africans and to avoid trouble with the British government, they encouraged Protestant immigration.

Indentured laborers, mostly white, dominated the Maryland workforce throughout the seventeenth century. As the laws infringing upon the rights and status of servitude for Africans grew more stringent in Virginia in the late seventeenth century, free Africans from Virginia, like Anthony and Mary Johnson and their family, migrated to Maryland. Enslavement was not absent in seventeenth century Maryland but it was not the principal form of servitude until the early eighteenth century (Yentsch 1994).

As the seventeenth century closed there were far fewer enslaved Africans in Maryland than in Virginia. In the four counties along the lower Western shore of Maryland, there were only 100 enslaved Africans in 1658, about 3% of the population. By 1710, their numbers had increased to 3500 making up about 24% of the population, most were still "country-born," that is born in Africa, and most were men. Between 1700 and 1780, new generations of African people born in the colony expanded the enslaved population (Menard 1975). [3]

CC licensed content, Shared previously

- **The American YAWP. Provided by**: Stanford University Press. **Located at**: http://www.americanyawp.com/index.html. **License**: *CC BY-SA: Attribution-ShareAlike*

Public domain content

- Park Ethnography Program. **Provided by**: National Park Service. **Located at**: https://www.nps.gov/ethnography/aah/aaheritage/histContextsA.htm. **Project**: African American Heritage and Ethnography. **License**: *Public Domain: No Known Copyright*

- Illustration titled Landing Negroes at Jamestown from Dutch man-of-war, 1619; signed H. Pyle. **Located at**: commons.wikimedia.org/wiki/File:AfricansatJamestown1619.jpg. **License**: *Public Domain: No Known Copyright*
- Illustration from 1670 showing African slaves curing and drying tobacco in the Virginia colony. **Located at**: commons.wikimedia.org/wiki/File:1670_virginia_tobacco_slaves.jpg. **License**: *Public Domain: No Known Copyright*
- Court Ruling on Anthony Johnson and His Servant. **Located at**: commons.wikimedia.org/wiki/File:Court_Ruling_on_Anthony_Johnson_and_His_Servant.png. **License**: *Public Domain: No Known Copyright*

3.3: Tightening the Bonds of Slavery

Tightening the Bonds of Slavery

In the early years of slavery, especially in Virginia and Maryland, the distinction between indentured servants and slaves was initially unclear. In 1643, however, a law was passed in Virginia that made African women "tithable." This, in effect, associated African women's work with difficult agricultural labor. There was no similar tax levied on white women; the law was an attempt to distinguish white from African women. The English ideal was to have enough hired hands and servants working on a farm so that wives and daughters did not have to partake in manual labor. Instead, white women were expected to labor in dairy sheds, small gardens, and kitchens. Of course, due to the labor shortage in early America, white women did participate in field labor. But this idealized gendered division of labor contributed to the English conceiving of themselves as better than other groups who did not divide labor in this fashion, including the West Africans arriving in slave ships to the colonies. For many white colonists, the association of a gendered division of labor with Englishness provided a further justification for the enslavement and subordination of Africans. [2]

Because of legislation in both Maryland and Virginia, life for those enslaved changed drastically in the 1660's. As European servants became scarce and expensive, African labor came to dominate the labor force. Legislation slowly sealed the fate of African immigrants and their descendants removing opportunities for freedom and advancement. Laws that made slavery hereditable came to pass in Virginia in 1662 and in Maryland in 1663. [3]

Virginia law's, for example, stated that an enslaved woman's children inherited the "condition" of their mother. This economic strategy on the part of planters created a legal system in which all children born to slave women would be slaves for life, whether the father was white or black, enslaved or free. These new laws also gave legal sanction to the enslavement of people of African descent for life. The permanent deprivation of freedom and the separate legal status of enslaved Africans facilitated the maintenance of strict racial barriers. Skin color became more than superficial difference; it became the marker of a transcendent, all-encompassing division between two distinct peoples, two races, white and black. [2]

The transformation of the "Negro" servant into the "Negro" slave was completed with the Virginia General Assembly passage of the *Slave Codes of 1705* . Thus, as the eighteenth century opened, most Africans and their American-born descendants lived and worked as slaves growing tobacco on "quarters" or "plantations" in rural, lower Chesapeake. They eventually improved their lives and by the 1720's, there were enough American-born Africans in Maryland to create their own African-American culture.

Inventories taken in Calvert, Charles, Prince George's and St. Mary's counties Maryland between 1658 and1710 found the slave population grew at an extraordinary rate increasing from about 100 enslaved people or 3% of the total counties' population in 1658 to over 3,500 people, composing 24% of the region's population in 1710. Almost all of these enslaved adults were African immigrants (Menard 1975:30–31). Within sixty-five years, almost all enslaved adults would be American-born, or as referred to here, African-Americans. [3]

Slave Life in the Eighteenth Century Chesapeake

Throughout the eighteenth century, most Africans came to the upper Chesapeake from two West African coast regions near what is today the nations of Sierra Leone, Liberia, Ivory Coast, and Ghana. (Walsh 1997:6). The continued importation of Africans from the same areas throughout the eighteenth century probably accounts for the fact that along with people born in African, many Maryland-born people of African descent continued to use African naming patterns. For example, a Maryland plantation's property inventory from 1734 lists a six-month-old child named Cusey, an African name. Cubit, Nom, Mingo or Tydoe are other African names found in the inventory. In other cases, Africans had English names that sounded like African names, for example: Jenny for Heminah, Patty for Pattoe or Sam for Samba. The Dulaney family's plantation inventories from 1720 to 1740 also included enslaved people with the African names: Toader, Abuer, Jam, Ockery, Hann, Southey, Cuffey, and Sango. (Yentsch 1994).

Most eighteenth-century Chesapeake Africans, and their native-born descendants, lived and worked as slaves growing tobacco on "quarters" or "plantations" in the eastern part of Virginia, although some were "industrial slaves" working at iron forges and others were hired out to work in gristmills and other industries. As plantation sizes increased, 40% or more of enslaved people lived in quarters away from the home plantation and the slave owner's direct supervision. On the largest plantations

people lived in small villages on "quarters" of the plantation holdings (See Figure 3-4). An enslaved man was often responsible for the work in the quarter that was designated by his name, such as "Mingo's Quarter." Relatively few enslaved people lived in urban areas with the slave owner's family.

By the last decades of the eighteenth century, 44% of the 46,547 enslaved people in the Chesapeake region lived in groups of more than 20 people in ten Tidewater counties: Anne Arundel, Prince George's, St. Mary's in Maryland and Essex, Gloucester, Lancaster, Middlesex, James City, Warwick, Charles City and York in Virginia. Another 34,000 enslaved people lived in similar sized groups on quarters or plantations in the Piedmont area of Virginia. (Kulikoff 1986:338).

Even though those in Maryland were more isolated and with limited social contact as compared to Virginian Africans, in both locales they formed families that slave owners recognized and recorded as family units in inventories (Menard 1975:33–37). Family and community formation was compromised from 1710 to 1730, the period of heaviest African immigration to the Chesapeake. During this time, African or "country-born" men, as they were called, competed with "native born" men for wives. Disproportionate sex ratios, resulting from the importation of greater numbers of African men than women, fostered internal conflicts and competition between African and African American men. In 1712, one African American complained "his country-men had poysened [sic] him for his wife." Another killed himself because he could not have more than one wife (Kulikoff 1986:334). At Carter's Grove plantation in 1733, "country-born" men lived in sex-segregated barracks. "Seasoned immigrants," as one historian refers to them, lived in conjugal units but without children, while native-born African Americans lived as families. These were optimal conditions. Native-born women at Carter's Grove preferred native-born men as husbands, limiting their opportunities for marriage.

A photograph from the 1930s showing an old slave quarter.Figure 3-4 — Old Quarters, Wisconsin Avenue & State Route 193, Bethesda, Montgomery County, MD by Thomas Waterman has no known copyright restriction.

Newly enslaved African-born women often waited two or three years before taking a husband (Kulikoff 1986). These personal preferences impeded formation of families.

Some families were polygamous, a sanctioned form of marriage in West Africa. Fictive kin families were formed of children sold onto a plantation community or left behind when their parents were sold or sent off to work in a far quarter of the plantation. Many enslaved people also participated in "abroad marriages," that is they were married to someone on another plantation or in another city. (Chambers 1996:121).

From 1736 to the end of the colonial period, kinship ties increasingly figured into enslaved people's decisions to run away, where they would run and with whom they would flee slavery. People ran away to their kin in other parts of the Chesapeake. The texts of some newspaper advertisements for runaways support the contention that knowledge Africans gained through travel must have been communicated throughout the African community and used to facilitate running away to distant places. In September 1776, James Scott, Jr. who lived in Fauquier County, Virginia, advertised in the Virginia Gazette for a woman

named Winney who in the past, as a runaway, traveled as far as "Maryland, near Port Tobacco, where she passed for a free woman, and hired herself in that neighbourhood [sic] several months."

By the end of the eighteenth century, the Chesapeake landscape was a network of large and small plantations. Although many planters on Maryland's western shore still held fewer than a dozen enslaved people, as the colonial period came to a close, African American family and kin-based social networks spread across several counties. [3]

3.4: Africans in the Low Country

Africans in the Low Country

Unlike the Virginia and Maryland colonies, the Carolina colony essentially imported a preexisting slave system from the Caribbean in the late seventeenth century. King Charles II of England chartered the Carolina colony in 1663 and it quickly developed a thriving economy based on African, African-American, and Native American slave labor. Nearly half of the colony's first white settlers came from Barbados in the eastern Caribbean where English landowners used African slaves on their sugarcane plantations. By the early 1700s, white plantation owners in Carolina relied almost exclusively on African and African-American slaves for labor on their rice and indigo plantations. Founded in 1670, Charles Town (later Charleston), soon became the colony's capital, a center of culture, commerce, and political power rooted in slavery. During the eighteenth century, more than half of all enslaved Africans who came to British North America would pass through the city. (Carson, *The Struggle for Freedom*, 54–55)

In 1712, Carolina split into two colonies, North and South Carolina (See Figure 3–5). Later, in 1733, James Oglethorpe settled the Georgia colony with a charter from King George the II to the land between the Savannah and Altamaha rivers. The Low Country, an area of fertile fields and swampy salt marshes, includes 79 barrier islands or "Sea Islands" along the Atlantic coast from southeastern North Carolina to the St. John River in northeast Florida.

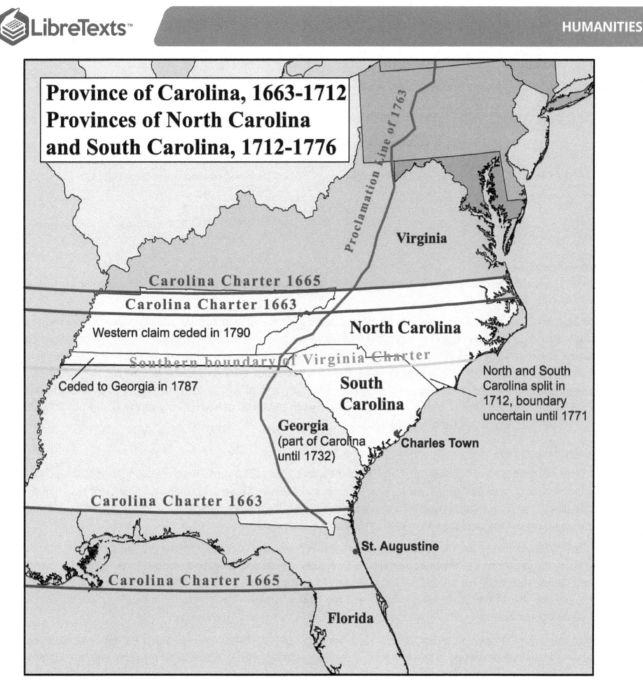

Province of Carolina, 1663-1712
Provinces of North Carolina
and South Carolina, 1712-1776

Map of the colonies of North and South Carolina and Georgia and their origin dates.Figure 3-5 — Carolinacolony by Kmusser is licensed under CC BY-SA 2.5

Rivers and tidewater streams lace the coastal plain creating widespread wetland landscapes. For Africans arriving in the Low Country, the climate and the wetlands, rivers and winding streams, if not the pine forests, must have seemed familiar, reminiscent of the landscapes they left behind in the wetlands of West or West Central Africa.

From the very earliest years of the colony, 20 to 30% of the settlers were Africans of diverse ethnic origins. During the first twenty-five years, about one in every four settlers was African. By 1720, Africans had outnumbered the Europeans for more than a decade. South Carolina was the one British colony in North America in which settlement and African slavery went hand in hand (Wood 1974; South Carolina 2004a).Over 40% of the Africans reaching the British colonies before the American Revolution passed through South Carolina. Almost all of these enslaved people entered the Charleston port. After a brief quarantine on Sullivan's Island they were sold in Charlestown, later called Charleston, slave markets (See Figure 3-6). Many of these enslaved people were almost immediately put to work in South Carolina's rice fields. Writers of the period remarked that there was no harder, or unhealthier, work possible. In fact, colonial travelers described the Carolina rice fields as charnel houses for enslaved African-Americans (Wood 1974; Morgan 1998).

Reproduction of a handbill advertising a slave auction, in Charleston, South Carolina, in 1769Figure 3-6 — Slave Auction Ad by Unknown is in the Public Domain .

In spite of the high death toll, a fortuitous combination of geographic and demographic factors, allowed these enslaved African peoples to shape their daily lives and customs according to African cultural traditions and to produce new African American cultural patterns. The first wave of Africans had more freedom to shape their culture than in any other part of the North American mainland (Morgan 1998:19). Not only did they live in autonomous units, in society as a whole, they made up a significantly large proportion of the population. As the eighteenth century opened Africans in South Carolina numbered 2,444, making up 75% of the total population. Within thirty years, there were 20,000 Africans, out-numbering Europeans 2:1. This was still the case in 1740. (Adams and Barnwell 2002). [3]

Rice Cultivation and Slavery in the Low Country

The second wave of African slaves brought to Carolina and Georgia after 1750 came from the Windward Coast of West Africa, a region stretching from Senegal down to Sierra Leone and Liberia. Traders acquired and sold Africans from this region because they came from rice growing cultures and brought with them technological and agricultural skills that were crucial to developing a thriving rice plantation system in the Low Country.

Geographer Judith Carney makes the case that Africans introduced sophisticated soil and water management techniques to Carolina and Georgia plantations. For tidal rice cultivation, an elaborate system of irrigation works—levees, ditches, culverts, floodgates, and drains—had to be constructed (and maintained) to control and regulate the flow of water onto and off of the fields. Carney explains that this agricultural technology and the hollow cypress logs known as "trunks" or "plugs," used to control water flow in embankments, were African innovations in Low Country rice cultivation.

In the ten years following the Stono Rebellion, a 1739 slave uprising near Charleston that resulted in the deaths of more than two dozen whites, the colony developed indigo as a second cash crop. Indigo, like rice, was labor intensive and its cultivation and processing for trade was well also known to Africans from the Windward Coast.

With both indigo and rice production depending upon the importation of Africans skilled in their cultivation and processing, economics won out over fear of more slave rebellions. In the aftermath of the Stono Rebellion in 1739, the South Carolina legislature began a ten year moratorium on the importation of slaves from Africa, which ended in 1750. Over 58,000 Africans entered South Carolina in the twenty-five years from 1750 and 1775 making South Carolina the largest direct importer of Africans for enslavement on the North American mainland. (Carney 2001:89). Over time, descendants of these early generations of Africans came to be known as the Gullah-Geechee people who had and continue to have distinctive cultural characteristics and a shared heritage.

Between 1730 and 1774, Low Country rice exports increased from 17 million pounds of rice annually to 66 million pounds. For the enslaved African people, particularly the women upon who successful rice production depended, there was an accompanying increase in hard labor and physical disability.

Rice cultivation and processing were mainly women's work. So it was in Africa and so it was on South Carolina and Georgia rice plantations. Enslaved men carried out skilled work making barrel staves for the crop's shipment. Men also monopolized blacksmithing, and cooperage and performed the hard work of preparing rice embankments and ditches (Carney 2001:199–

120). Ultimately, however, it was the labor of African women and their daughters that made the phenomenal growth of the Low Country rice economy possible (See Figure 3-7).

Figure 3-7 — Rice Culture on the Ogeechee, near Savannah, Georgia by A.R. Waud is in the Public Domain .

African women brought three rice cultivation techniques to Low Country plantations: sowing in trenched ground, open trench planting, and tidal rice cultivation. A description of enslaved people's preparation of rice for open trench planting in the nineteenth century corresponds with the contemporary rice planting system in Sierra Leone in West Africa as well as with descriptions of late eighteenth early nineteenth centuries methods used in South Carolina:

Young men brought the clay water in piggies[sic] from the barrel and poured it over the rice, while young girls, with bare feet and skirts well tied up, danced and shuffled the rice about with their feet until the whole mass was thoroughly clayed,…When it is completely covered with clay, the rice is shovelled [sic] into a pyramid and left to soak until the next morning, when it is measured out into sacks, one and one-fourth bushels to each half acre…(Pringle 1914:375–376).

Enslaved women pressed the rice seeds into the muddy ground with their heels. Afterwards men called "trunk minders" flooded the fields to encourage seed germination.

"It is literally casting one's bread on the waters … for as soon as the seed is in the ground the trunk door is lifted and the water creeps slowly up and up until it is about three inches deep on the land. That is why the claying is necessary; it makes the grain adhere to the earth, otherwise it would float (Pringle 1914:12–13)."

Once the seeds sprouted, enslaved men drained the fields and the women weeded them. Weeding the rice fields had to be done by hand. The fields were then alternately flooded and drained to keep the soil moist and the weeds under control, and to deter the birds and other animals. The final flooding took place under the watchful eye of the "trunk minder," who was responsible for gradually raising the water level in the fields to support the top-heavy rice stalk.

After harvesting the rice, allowing for a short period during which it dried, the enslaved women processed the rice. First, they threshed the rice to remove the rice grains from the stalks. Threshing entailed beating the rice with a stick or having the farm animals trampling the stalks. Next, they pounded the rice using a hand-pounding mortar and pestle to separate the indigestible hulls from the rice.

Pounding rice required great skill to insure that the majority of the end product was clean whole grains rather than partially broken or small broken pieces of rice. African women were highly skilled in pounding rice. However, processing rice for subsistence use as they had done in their West African homeland was quite different from processing rice as a cash crop.

Pounding rice was grueling work. In West Africa, women pounded enough rice for a family's meals. In the Low Country, throughout the eighteenth century, enslaved women pounded about 44 pounds of rice a day, cumulatively millions of pounds of rice for export.

After pounding, they then poured the rice onto a fanner for winnowing. Then they removed the indigestible hulls, or chafe, by tossing the rice up and down in the wide shallow fanner basket. During this process the basket was gently tilted back and forth, tossing the rice upward and outward, allowing the husk to be blown away by the wind. (Careny 2001)

In eighteenth century South Carolina, African women made the winnowing baskets from light grasses and palmetto leaf. Anthropologist Dale Rosengarten has established that the weaving style of winnowing baskets and the process of winnowing passed down from South Carolina slaves to their Low Country-born African Americans descendants, are West African, not Native American, in origin (Rosengarten, 1986; Carney 2001:114). Coiled grass baskets are a tradition in many parts of West Africa. Descendants of enslaved Africans who came to the Low Country made baskets for winnowing and other purposes in the 1700s, and the tradition continues among many Low Country African-Americans today.

After harvest, men and women both worked to prepare the fields for the next rice crop. This was arduous work but none was as arduous as processing the millions of pounds of rice for shipment overseas, mostly within a few months when the crop was in greatest demand.

As onerous as pounding seven mortars of rice or splitting 100 poles for fences, trenching, hoeing, or plowing $1/4$ to a $1/2$ acre of land per day must have been, the burden was mitigated by the knowledge that at the end of the task was "free time." The task system of work assignment was perhaps the most distinctive and central feature of enslaved African life in the Low Country. By the end of the eighteenth century, the task system was firmly entrenched from South Carolina to Florida, wherever rice was cultivated, and planters extended the system to organization of labor in raising Sea Island cotton.

Under the task system, a person was assigned a certain amount of work for the day after which he or she could use their time as they pleased (Morgan 1982:566). "Owning" time, making one's own decisions, owning the products of one's labor, were powerful ideas, empowering incentives and in the end led to positive outcomes for enslaved low country Africans.

After they [slaves] finished "their required day's work, they were given as much land as they could handle on which they planted corn, potatoes, tobacco, peanuts, sugar, watermelons, and pumpkins and bottle pumpkins... They plant for themselves on Sundays...They sell their own crops and buy some necessary things..." wrote Johan Bolzius of low country slaves in the mid-18 [th] century (Bolzius 1750:259–60, Translated and edited by Loewald, Starika and Taylor, 1957).

Once gained, "free" time expanded allowing enslaved people not only the opportunity to tend their own crops but also to socialize, grow and sell surplus products, gain personal property through such sales and ultimately to accumulate money to purchase their own freedom and that of their family members.

In South Carolina a series of laws passed between 1686 and 1751 reflect the growing concern of slave holders over the ways in which the Africans chose to spend their "own time." A 1686 law prohibited the exchange of goods between slaves or slaves and freemen without their master's permission. Ten years later the lawmakers tried to prohibit slaves felling and carrying away timber on lands other than their masters. In 1714, the legislature prohibited that "slaves plant for themselves any corn, peas, or rice," apparently to no avail since 20 years later another act was passed allowing patrollers to confiscate all fowls and other provisions found in the possession of "stragling [sic] negroes." Many planters came to depend upon the foods, goods and services provided to them by the Africans. At best, their dependency must have made them ambivalent about enforcing the prohibitive laws.

Low Country slaves raised crops that reflected their African origins such as okra, groundnuts (peanuts) sesame seed, called Benni, and "Read {sic} peppers." African vegetables and rice became part of the staple diet of new generations of African Americans and were eaten by planters as well. Both Elias Ball and Eliza Lucas Pinckney mention, for example, "negro" grown peppers in their letters (Morgan 1982:574). Enslaved entrepreneurs branched out from huckstering foods to making and selling other commodities such as canoes, baskets and wax (Ball, 1837).

Over time, enslaved people used surplus income from the internal economy to buy livestock, including horses, and one at least negotiated his own freedom (Morgan 1982:580). After completing their tasks for the slave master, the African men hunted,

fished, worked as carpenters and in other trades to earn money. The women washed clothes, prepared food and cooked for their families, raised chickens and vegetables to eat and to sell. These activities allow the Africans to participate in trade and cash sales through which some men and women earned and saved money to buy themselves and their kin out of slavery. By the time of the Revolutionary War, two or more generations of native-born African Americans, had a variety of occupational skills that they used to earn enough money to buy freedom. However, even those who continued enslavement gained a degree of autonomy through internal economies that developed throughout the colonies. [3]

Conclusion

By late eighteenth century, before the colonies convulsed during the American Revolution, racial slavery had become rooted in the soil and law of colonies stretching from Georgia north to New England. But nowhere was slavery more important to British North American economy than in the Chesapeake colonies of Virginia and Maryland, and the Low Country colonies of South Carolina and Georgia. The extraordinary wealth African and African-American slaves produced for white plantation owners not only created an economic aristocracy, but a political ruling class who also cherished the liberty and freedom slave labor made possible for them.

As colonists began to revolt against British rule during the 1760s and 1770s, they often viewed their plight through the lens of slavery. They saw Parliament's infringement upon their rights and privileges as British subjects as akin to enslavement and many colonial leaders in turn used the language of natural rights, of liberty and freedom, in their fight for independence from Britain.

During the American Revolution, many African-American slaves would seize upon this language to demand their own freedom from slavery. Others would flee their masters during the chaos of war and fight alongside the British against the rebellious colonists or else join the patriot cause and fight in the Continental Army and Navy in hope of securing their freedom at the end of the war. Regardless of the side they fought on, African-Americans forced whites to confront the ironies and contradictions of fighting a revolution in the name of natural rights and liberty while choosing to maintain slavery. [1]

CHAPTER OVERVIEW

4: AFRICAN AMERICANS AND THE AMERICAN REVOLUTION

4.1: Introduction

African Americans and the American Revolution

Module Introduction

"How is it that we hear the loudest yelps for liberty among the drivers of Negroes?" Samuel Johnson, the great English writer and dictionary maker, posed this question in 1775, the year the American Revolutionary War broke out. He was among the first, but certainly not the last, to contrast the noble aims of the American Revolution with the presence of 450,000 enslaved black men, women, and children in the 13 colonies. [4]In America, the freedom of some, it seemed, was inextricably linked to the enslavement of others. The creation of a system of racial slavery not only generated wealth for plantation owners, merchants, and traders, it secured the freedom and liberty of whites colonists. The presence of slavery created a common bond among white colonists regardless of their origin and class. As European indentured servitude declined in America during the eighteenth century, whites, regardless of their socio-economic status, shared a racial identity that guaranteed their freedom and legal superiority over black people. Whiteness became associated with freedom and liberty, including independence from being a slave or a servant. Blackness became associated with dependence, bondage, and racial inferiority. White freedom was thus dependent on black slavery. [1]

During the Revolutionary era in America (1765–1783), black people, both slave and free, questioned and resisted the logic and legality of slavery and racial inequality. They understood and harnessed the language of natural rights, including those "yelps for liberty" that whites used in their revolt against British colonial rule. Black people made claims to these rights by petitioning courts for their freedom, by joining or forming anti-slavery societies, by running away from their masters, and by fighting for their freedom in both the British and American armies during the Revolutionary War. The Revolution was a war for freedom and equality for African Americans rather than simply independence from Great Britain. Their actions forced Americans to debate the morality and legality of slavery, and its compatibility with revolutionary ideals. America's social and economic investment in racial slavery was too deeply rooted to remove, however. Slavery not only survived the Revolution but continued to thrive and spread like a virus into new lands in the west and the Deep South in the ensuing years and decades. [1]

Learning Outcomes

This module addresses the following Course Learning Outcomes listed in the Syllabus for this course:

- To provide students with a general understanding of the history of African Americans within the context of American History
- To motivate students to become interested and active in African American history by comparing current events with historical information

Additional learning outcomes associated with this module are:

- The student will be able to discuss the origins, evolution, and spread of racial slavery.
- The student will be able to describe the creation of a distinct African-American culture and how that culture became part of the broader American culture.
- The student will be able to describe how African-Americans, during times of war, have forced America to live up to its promise of freedom and equality. [1]

Module Objectives

Upon completion of this module, the student will be able to:

Use primary historical documents to explain why and how black people used the language of revolution and natural rights in petition for freedoma nd the abolition of slavery. [1]

Readings and Resources

- Learning Unit: African Americans and the American Revolution (see below) [1]
- Primary Historical Documents

  o *Petition of Slaves in Boston, Province of Massachusetts Bay* by Felix
  o Freedom Petition of Prince Hall

CC licensed content, Shared previously

4.2: African Americans and the Rhetoric of Revolution

African Americans and the American Revolution

African Americans and the Rhetoric of Revolution

Thomas Jefferson, and other leaders of the Revolution, studied and borrowed ideas of natural rights from European Enlightenment philosophers such as John Locke. They then incorporated natural rights theory into documents like the Declaration of Independence that not only justified the Revolution but served, in Jefferson's words, as "an expression of the American mind." Natural rights, such as the right to be free and pursue one's own "happiness," are rights all human beings possess that are not granted by government and cannot be revoked or repealed. As it says in the preamble to the Declaration of Independence, natural rights are "truths" that are "self-evident" and "unalienable" such as "life, liberty, and the pursuit of happiness."

How could a group of people feel so passionate about these unalienable rights, yet maintain the brutal practice of human bondage? Somehow slavery would manage to survive the revolutionary era despite fervent arguments about its incompatibility with the new nation's founding ideals.[5] Nevertheless, black people in particular seized on the rhetoric of the American Revolution to highlight the contradiction between the colonists' cries for freedom and liberty from British oppression and the existence of racial slavery in the colonies. [1]

African Americans, both slave and free, immediately jumped into the fray when white colonists began to protest British colonial rule for the first time in 1765 in response to the Stamp Act, which imposed a tax on newspapers, pamphlets, and legal documents. Many colonists viewed the act as an arbitrary tax designed only to generate revenue to pay down debt Britain accrued during the French and Indian War, which colonists helped the British win in the 1750s and 1760s. Colonists also resented that this tax was imposed on them without having a voice in Parliament, which led to cries of "No taxation without representation!"

In Charleston, South Carolina, slaves saw white protesters take to the streets and chant, "Liberty! Liberty! And stamp'd paper." The issue of taxation, of course, mattered far less to slaves than the language whites used in their protests. Soon after Charleston's white residents protested the Stamp Act, some of the city's slaves responded with their own chants of "Liberty! Liberty!," which shocked and frightened white residents. "If most slaves were illiterate," writes historian David Brian Davis, "white leaders knew or soon discovered that the slaves' networks of communication passed on every kind of news almost as quickly as horses could gallop." (Davis, 2006, p.144–146)

A visual protest against the Stamp Act printed in a colonial American newspaper.Figure 4-1: O! the fatal stamp by Pennsylvania Journal is in the Public Domain .

African Americans, and some whites opposed to slavery, also recognized the curious irony of statements made by some white colonists that characterized British policies as a conspiracy that threatened to turn free white people into "slaves," that is, people lacking the same rights and liberties as British citizens overseas. In 1774, George Washington characterized the plight of colonists under British rule as analogous to that of black slaves ruled over by white slaves masters like himself. Writing after Parliament passed the Intolerable Acts to punish rebellious colonists for the Boston Tea Party, Washington said, "the crisis is arrived when we must assert our rights, or submit to every imposition, that can be heaped upon us, till custom and use shall make us tame and abject slaves, as the blacks we rule over with such arbitrary sway." (Jordan, 1968, p. 262)

At the time, Washington was a political leader in Virginia and the master of a large plantation along the Potomac River, Mt. Vernon, where he personally owned more than one hundred slaves. In the late 1760s, the famous Philadelphia physician, Benjamin Rush, wrote a correspondent in France about how the Revolution's rhetoric of liberty and freedom, and the potential for enslavement or servitude, forced American colonists to reckon with the hypocrisy of fighting for liberty and rights while countenancing racial slavery. "It would be useless for us to denounce the servitude to which the Parliament of Great Britain wishes to reduce us, while we continue to keep our fellow creatures in slavery just because their color is different from ours." (Davis, 2006, p. 145).

George Washington and his family depicted at Washington's Mt. Vernon plantation home in Virginia.Figure 4-2: The Washington Family by Edward Savage is in the Public Domain .

In 1773, Phyllis Wheatley, an eighteen-year-old poet who had been born in West Africa but now lived as a slave in Massachusetts, reflected on the same contradictions Rush highlighted a few years earlier. "In every human Breast, God has implanted a Principle, which we call Love of Freedom," Wheatley wrote. How then can white colonists reconcile the "Cry of Liberty" with the "Exercise of Oppressive Power over others?" (Carson, Lapansky-Werner & Nash, 2019, p. 94)

That same year, which saw a record number of antislavery pamphlets published and sermons given in the America colonies, a slave named Felix sent a freedom petition on behalf of himself and other slaves in Massachusetts to the colonial governor and legislature. Freedom petitions, or freedom suits, had existed in the American colonies since the late 1600s and allowed slaves to ask courts or legislatures to free them from bondage on the basis of legal violations. While a small number of slaves petitioned courts for their freedom, the number of petitions rose during the American Revolution. In his petition, Felix argued that slavery left black people in bondage for life without the hope of acquiring property and freedom for themselves or their progeny. No matter how devoted slaves were to their masters "neither they, nor their Children to all Generations, shall ever be able to do so, or to possess and enjoy any Thing, no, not even Life itself, but in a Manner as the Beasts that perish." Since the law deprived slaves of property and instead made them into property, their condition resembled that of an animal and not a human being. This was a violation of natural rights. "Relief" from the legislature of Massachusetts that would not harm their masters, and free them from slavery, would be "to us… as Life from the dead." (Davis, 2006, p. 146)

Black Americans continued to petition for their freedom during the Revolutionary War, which broke out in 1775 in Massachusetts, while others free blacks protested on behalf of the enslaved by highlighting the contradictions between a war fought for freedom and the persistence of slavery. In 1777, a former slave, named Prince Hall, declared that the ideals Americans fought for "in the course of their unhappy difficulties with Great Britain pleads stronger than a thousand arguments… [that black people] may be restored to the enjoyments of that which is the natural right of all men." (Carson, Lapansky-Werner & Nash, 2019, p. 94). Two years earlier, Hall founded the first African American branch of Freemasonry and started the first black Masonic Lodge in Boston. [1]

Copper Engraving of Phyllis Wheatley that appears in her book of poetry, Poems on Various Subjects, Religious and Moral, which was published in 1773.Figure 4-3: Phyllis Wheatley frontispiece by Scipio Moorhead is in the Public Domain .

Thomas Jefferson

No one embodied the contradictions that lay at the heart of the Revolution's rhetoric more than Thomas Jefferson. Like George Washington, Jefferson was part of Virginia's slaveholding aristocracy. Slavery afforded Jefferson the opportunity and freedom to pursue a career as a lawyer and political leader in Virginia before and during the American Revolution. When the Revolution broke out, Jefferson owned just under 200 slaves on his central Virginia plantation, Monticello. As a student of the European Enlightenment, and a scholar of treatises on natural rights written by Enlightenment philosophers such as John Locke, Jefferson saw slavery as a regrettable institution and hoped a process of gradual emancipation would eventually lead to its permanent demise.

When Jefferson wrote the Declaration of Independence in the summer of 1776, he used the language of natural rights to justify the revolution and, in so doing, composed some of the most important, and potentially radical, words in American history that carried anti-slavery overtones:

We hold these truths to be self-evident, that all men are created equal, that there are endowed by the Creator with certain unalienable Rights, that among these are Life, Liberty, and the pursuit of Happiness. (US, 1776)

Since he was writing about natural rights, and not political or civil rights, Jefferson saw this equality and desire for freedom and "happiness" (i.e. property) as applying to all people, even Africans and African Americans. Jefferson made this belief clear in a passage he wrote in an early draft of the Declaration that was eventually removed because it threatened the support of the states of South Carolina and Georgia in the cause of independence. In this passage, Jefferson blamed the African slave trade and slavery on King George rather than on colonial slaveholders like himself. King George, he argued, "has waged cruel war against human nature itself, violating the most sacred rights of life & liberty in the persons of a distant people [i.e. Africans] who never offended him, captivating & carrying them into slavery in another hemisphere, or to incur miserable death in their transportation thither." (Davis, 2006, p. 146)

Despite Jefferson's recognition that slavery violated the natural rights of Africans and African Americans, he only freed a very small number of his slaves during his life and left hundreds still in bondage at his death in 1826. After the Revolution, Jefferson recognized that an explanation was in order. How could the author of the Declaration of Independence, one of the most eloquent statements of the natural rights of all people, not free his own slaves or advocate for the immediate abolition of slavery? Jefferson wrote his explanation in his only published book, *Notes on the State of Virginia* (1782). In Jefferson's mind, abolition carried grave threats and risks to the young United States. He envisioned an apocalyptic race war in which former slaves would slaughter former slave owners out of revenge. He also borrowed pseudo-scientific racist ideas from the European Enlightenment that argued that Africans were inferior to Europeans, particularly in terms of intellectual capacities, which made them unfit as citizens.

"Deep rooted prejudices entertained by the whites; ten thousand recollections, by the blacks, of the injuries they have sustained; new provocations; the real distinctions which nature has made; and many other circumstances, will divide us into parties, and produce convulsions which will probably never end but in the extermination of the one or the other race," Jefferson wrote.

He also feared racial "mixture" and the corruption of white racial purity, despite maintaining a sexual relationship with his slave, Sally Hemings, a woman who bore him five children and who herself was the product of a sexual encounter between Jefferson's father-in-law and Hemings's mother, Betty. Jefferson still hoped emancipation would happen at some distant date in the future and when it occurred all former slaves will have to be "removed beyond the reach of mixture." For Jefferson, the author of the Declaration of Independence, eventual emancipation could only occur with a plan for the colonization of African Americans outside of the United States where they could have their own country separate from white Americans. [1]

A caricature of Thomas Jefferson and Sally Hemings.Figure 4-4: A Philosophic Cock attributed to James Akin is in the Public Domain .

CC licensed content, Original

- **Authored by**: Florida State College at Jacksonville. **License**: *CC BY: Attribution*

CC licensed content, Shared previously

- U.S. History. **Provided by**: The Independence Hall Association. **Located at**: http://www.ushistory.org/us/index.asp. **License**: *CC BY: Attribution*

Public domain content

- O! the fatal stamp. **Provided by**: Pennsylvania Journal. **Located at**: commons.wikimedia.org/wiki/File:O!_the_fatal_Stamp.jpg. **License**: *Public Domain: No Known Copyright*
- The Washington Family. **Authored by**: Edward Savage. **Located at**: commons.wikimedia.org/wiki/File:The_Washington_Family_by_Edward_Savage_1798.jpg. **License**: *Public Domain: No Known Copyright*
- Phyllis Wheatley frontispiece. **Authored by**: Scipio Moorhead. **Located at**: commons.wikimedia.org/wiki/File:Phillis_Wheatley_frontispiece.jpg. **License**: *Public Domain: No Known Copyright*
- A Philosophic Cock. **Authored by**: James Akin. **Located at**: commons.wikimedia.org/wiki/File:Cock_ca1804_attrib_to_JamesAkin_AmericanAntiquarianSociety.png. **License**: *Public Domain: No Known Copyright*

4.3: Fighting Their Way to Freedom

Fighting Their Way to Freedom

In addition to filing freedom petitions and writing pamphlets advocating for the abolition of slavery, African Americans fought for their freedom during the colonial and revolutionary era by serving in the military. African and African American men, enslaved and free, from the South and the North, served in every war of consequence during the colonial period. Sometimes slaveholders sent enslaved men to the front to fight in their place or to do the menial labor entailed in building fortifications and supporting fighting troops. In other cases, African runaways posed as free persons in order to serve on ships or to enlist as soldiers. The newspapers of the colonial period often mention these facts in their advertisements of fugitive slaves.

Before the Revolution, between 1675 and 1739, the southern colonies were almost constantly involved in fighting Native Americans or the Spanish. Southern planters were hesitant about arming Africans, as evidenced by the legislation they passed prohibiting "Negro[es], mulatto[s] or Indian[s] from the military or bearing arms."

However, expedience required that equally as often the Virginians and South Carolina planters recruited black men to fight in a militia or serve as "pioneers", or "slave cowboys" to protect their settlements. In 1703, the South Carolina assembly offered to free any slave who captured or killed hostile Native Americans. Beginning as early as 1705, free blacks became eligible for enrollment in the militia. Unlike white persons, they were required to muster for service without bringing arms. Several acts passed by the colonial assembly between 1723 and 1757, said that black men could serve as drummers, fifers, trumpeters, or "pioneers," but not as regular soldiers (Jackson 1942:251). The rank of "pioneer" gave them a special place as laborers and menial servants. Many were freed for their services, but not all.

During the Revolutionary War some Africans and African Americans fought on the side of the patriots while others fought on the side of the Loyalists. All enslaved people fought in order to gain freedom. [3]

Black Loyalists in the Revolutionary War

A member of Dunmore's "Ethiopian" or black regiment that fought for the British or loyalist side during the Revolutionary War.Figure 4-5: Ethiopian Regiment Uniform by Bantarleton is licensed under CC BY-SA 4.0.

The British made the first move to enlist black soldiers. In November 1775, Lord Dunmore, the British colonial governor of Virginia, issued a proclamation that all slaves belonging to rebels would be received into the British forces and freed for their services. African Americans ran away to fight with the British in search of promised freedom for their services. Dunmore organized an "Ethiopian" regiment of about 300 African Americans, who saw action at the Battle of Great Bridge in December 1775. [4]

The hope of freedom in return for service led many enslaved African Americans to leave the plantation to follow the British Army. No exact statistics are available on the number of enslaved people who reached British sanctuaries, but Thomas Jefferson estimated the number at 30,000 in 1778 alone (Tate 1865:119). In South Carolina, some 5,000 enslaved people left the plantation to follow the British. The British confiscated other enslaved people from patriots. The British organized the Africans following them as laborers, paying them small sums in principal, although they charged them for clothes and upkeep, thus leaving them with little actual monetary gain. The act of paying for labor defused the potential for rebellion and led to many courageous acts on the part of black people.

During the final months of the British Occupation of South Carolina, in 1781, General Leslie Clark formed black men into unit called Leslie's "Black Dragoons."

From the patriots' point of view, one historian comments, "The knowledge that hundreds of self-liberated slaves were in possession of weapons caused resentment and detestation (Frey 1991:125–167)." The British went on to form autonomous "Negro" units for service in Florida and the West Indies. Their service convinced others that the best solution to British military problems in the West Indies was to enlist slaves by offering them freedom. The British subsequently sent black regiments for service in Saint Domingue during the French Revolution and Napoleonic Wars (Frey 1991). [3]

At the war's end in 1783, some 20,000 blacks left with the British, preferring an uncertain future elsewhere to returning to their old masters and plantations. [4] They hoped that the British government would uphold the promise of freedom and help them establish new homes elsewhere in the Empire. The Treaty of Paris, which ended the war, demanded that British troops leave runaway slaves behind, but the British military commanders upheld earlier promises and evacuated thousands of freedmen, transporting them to Canada, the Caribbean, or Great Britain. They would eventually play a role in settling Nova Scotia, and through the subsequent efforts of David George, a black loyalist and Baptist preacher, some settled in Sierra Leone, in Africa. Black loyalists, however, continued to face social and economic marginalization, including restrictions on land ownership within the British Empire. [2]

Black Patriots in the Revolutionary War

In the 1850s, the free black abolitionist, William C. Nell of Boston, published the nation's first histories of African Americans that addressed the military service on the Patriot side during the American Revolution. In his 1855 publication, *Colored Patriots of the American Revolution* , he singled out Crispus Attucks, a black man of African and Native American ancestry who worked on whaling ships in Massachusetts, as the first man to die in the American fight for independence. Five years before war broke out between colonists and Britain, Attucks had been one of five Americans killed in the Boston Massacre on March 5, 1770. Attucks became something of martyr and a symbol of British oppression. A century after the massacre, a Massachusetts poet honored and memorialized Attucks in a long poem that praised him as the "first to defy, and the first to die." (Carson, Lapansky-Werner & Nash, 2019, p.98) [1]

A lithograph created by John Bufford made during the mid-nineteenth century depicting the Boston Massacre of 1770. Crispus Attucks is shown in the center foreground of the image after being shot by a British solider.Figure 4-6: Boston Massacre by John H. Bufford is in the Public Domain .

Despite the patriotic fervor Attucks's death may have inspired, far fewer black people fought alongside the Americans against the British during the Revolutionary War. Nevertheless, some black men in New England rallied to the patriot cause and were part of the militia forces that were organized into the new Continental Army. Approximately 5 percent of the American soldiers at the Battle of Bunker Hill (June 17, 1775) were black. New England blacks mostly served in integrated units and received the same pay as whites, although none held a rank higher than corporal.

Historians estimate that about 5,000 black soldiers ultimately fought on the patriot side. The exact number will never be known because eighteenth century muster rolls usually did not indicate race. Careful comparisons between muster rolls and church, census, and other records have recently helped identify many black soldiers. Additionally, various eyewitness accounts provide some indication of the level of African Americans' participation during the war. Baron von Closen, a member of Rochambeau's French army at Yorktown, wrote in July 1781, "A quarter of them [the American army] are Negroes, merry, confident and sturdy."

The use of black men as soldiers, whether freemen or slaves, was avoided early in the war by Congress and George Washington, General of the Continental Army. The prospect of armed slave revolts proved more threatening to white American society than British redcoats. General Washington allowed the enlistment of free blacks with "prior military experience" in January 1776, and extended the enlistment terms to all free blacks in January 1777 in order to help fill the depleted ranks of the Continental Army. Because the states constantly failed to meet their quotas of manpower for the army, Congress authorized the enlistment of all blacks, free and slave, in 1777. Of the southern states, only Maryland permitted African Americans to enlist. In 1779, Congress offered slave masters in South Carolina and Georgia $1,000 for each slave they

provided to the army, but the legislatures of both states refused the offer. Thus, the greatest number of black soldiers in the American army came from the North.

Although most Continental regiments were integrated, a notable exception was the elite First Rhode Island. Mustered into service in July 1778, the First Rhode Island numbered 197 black enlisted men commanded by white officers. Baron von Closen described the regiment as "the most neatly dressed, the best under arms, and the most precise in its maneuvers." The regiment received its baptism of fire at the battle of Rhode Island (Newport) on August 29, 1778, successfully defeating three assaults by veteran Hessian troops. At the siege of Yorktown, on the night of October 14, 1781, the regiment's light company participated in the assault and capture of Redoubt 10. On June 13, 1783, the regiment was disbanded, receiving high praise for its service. Another notable black unit, recruited in the French colony of St. Domingue (present-day Haiti), fought with the French and patriots at the Battle of Savannah (October 9, 1779). [4]

In Maryland the other part of the Chesapeake region, black men were not considered to be among the optional sources for filling quotas in the Continental Army or the militia units until enlistment shortfalls made it expedient to broaden the base of eligible persons. A "Return of the Negroes in the Army, August 24, 1778" indicates there were about 95 "Negroes" among the Maryland troops. However, finding the identification of these men is difficult because they were rarely identified by race on muster rolls. By 1780 Maryland was ready to accept enlistments from any source and more "negroes" enlisted. In 1781 Charles Carroll wrote his father "we shall pass a law tomorrow for raising a Negro regiment of 750—every person having six Negroes between fourteen and forty-five years of age may have a Negro taken from him if the Negro should be willing to enlist for the war (Maryland State Archives, 84:297 as cited by Kreinheder and Schmidt 2001:121).

The North Carolina General Assembly initiated a draft in 1777 providing "that all men within the ages of 16 and 50 were liable to serve…[in the Continental Army]…or find an able bodied man to take their place" There were no color qualifications made in the act. The fact that men of "mixed colors" participated in North Carolina military units is evident from many sources (Schmidt 2001:159).

Georgia, not even 50 years a colony at the onset of the War, had about 18,000 enslaved people in its population even though they declared their "abhorrence of the unnatural practice on slavery," in their 1775 declaration of support for the patriots in Boston and Massachusetts and for the Revolutionary War to come. Georgia used the conflict to try to improve relationships with Native Americans in the colony. The Georgia records of minorities' service in the military are not always clear. The National Society of the daughters of the American Revolution authenticated records identify four "Black" soldiers and one "Indian" soldier from Georgia (2001:1181–182). The Revolutionary War was not exclusively a "Man's World." Four women have been authenticated in southern colonial records of Africans and Indians serving in the Revolutionary War. Sarah, a "Black" woman, worked in the lead mines of Virginia, Catherine the Grenadier, also known as the Shawnee woman, served in the Continental Army as did Nancy Ward another Native American woman from North Carolina. Patty was a "Black" seamstress, whose name is found in the papers of Henry Laurens, performed military service for South Carolina (African American and American Indian Patriots of the American Revolution, 2001:148, 153,166, 182).

After the war, the black soldiers and seamen of Virginia were liberally rewarded in money, land bounties, and granted them pensions. In common with other states, Virginia also provided for the manumission of some slaves who fought. However, they had to petition the courts to gain freedom and were not successful until ten or more years after the struggle. In the next century, the children of African American Revolutionary War veterans who did not receive land, petitioned the State of Virginia for land, and received it (Jackson 1942). [3]

- The American Revolution. **Provided by**: National Park Service. **Located at**: https://www.nps.gov/revwar/index.html. **License**: *Public Domain: No Known Copyright*
- Boston Massacre. **Authored by**: John H. Bufford. **Located at**: commons.wikimedia.org/wiki/File:Boston_Massacre,_03-05-1770_-_NARA_-_518262.jpg. **License**: *Public Domain: No Known Copyright*

4.4: The Impact of the Revolution on Slavery

The Impact of the Revolution on Slavery

The American Revolution generated unprecedented debates about morality of slavery and its compatibility with the founding creeds of the new nation. Though the Revolution did not lead to abolition of slavery, it set off a process of both immediate and gradual emancipation in northern states. The South's slave system suffered because of the war, which resulted in a decline in production and a loss of thousands of slaves to the British. Though a small number of slaveholders, particularly in Virginia, emancipated their slaves after the Revolution, slavery remained entrenched in the southern states and would only become more profitable and spread further to the west and south during the late eighteenth and into the nineteenth century.

In 1775, the year the Revolutionary War began, Quakers founded the world's first antislavery society in Philadelphia, Pennsylvania. Quakers, also known as the Society of Friends, are a pacifist Christian sect that believe all humans possess an inner light, that God dwells inside everyone. Consequently, most Quakers have espoused historically controversial ideas of racial and gender equality, and viewed slavery as an immoral and dehumanizing institution, despite the fact that some Quakers still owned slaves before the Revolution. Following the Quaker's example, at least thirteen of anti-slavery societies came into existence in America by 1788. [5]

The fight for liberty led some American slaveholders to free their slaves, and most northern states soon passed gradual emancipation laws. [2] In 1777, Vermont created a new state constitution that outlawed slavery making it first place in the New World to do so. Six years later, Massachusetts and New Hampshire also outlawed slavery through judicial decisions. Further to the south, Pennsylvania passed a law outlining a process of gradual emancipation that said that the children born after March 1, 1780 to mothers who were slaves would be considered indentured servants and be completely free from their masters when they turned 28. New York and New Jersey, where slavery was more prevalent, did not pass gradual emancipation laws until 1799 and 1804, respectively. (Davis, 2006) While the state of Delaware would not abolish slavery until the passage of the Thirteenth Amendment in 1865, 31 percent of its African American population were free by 1790 because of the anti-slavery activism of Quakers and Methodists. (Carson, 2019)

Some manumissions also occurred in the Upper South, most notably in Virginia. In 1782, near the end of the Revolution, the Virginia Assembly passed a law that removed restrictions on masters to free their slaves. The next year, the Assembly freed any slaves who had fought on behalf of the Continental Army during the war. These new laws led to the rapid growth of Virginia's free black population. In 1780, there were 2,800 free black people and by 1810 there were 30,000 living in Virginia. Virginia also banned the foreign importation of slaves in 1778, though more out of fear of a growing black population and concern that a large surplus of slaves would diminish the market value of those the state's slaveholders already owned. (Ford, 2009) [1]

On the other hand, the Lower South, particularly South Carolina and Georgia, remained passionately committed to the African slave trade and some masters in the region revoked their offers of freedom for war service while others forced freed black people back into bondage. [2]

Perhaps the most significant step to address the issue of slavery taken by the Continental Congress under the Articles of Confederation, and before the ratification of the new United States Constitution, was the passage of the Northwest Ordinance in 1787, which organized new territory west of the Appalachian Mountains and north of the Ohio River. The Northwest Ordinance also prohibited slaveholders from bring in slaves into the Northwest Territory while permitting slaveholders who already lived in the area to maintain their human property. (Carson, Lapansky-Werner & Nash, 2019) [1]

A map that shows the land in black designated as the Northwest Territory by the Northwest Ordinance of 1787. The map also shows the years that individual territories in the region were admitted into the union as states.Figure 4-7: Northwest territory usa 1787 by Unknown is licensed under CC BY-SA 3.0 Unported .

The Revolution's rhetoric of equality also created a "revolutionary generation" of slaves and free black Americans that would eventually galvanize the antislavery movement well into the nineteenth century. [2] The growing class of free blacks established their own social institutions including churches, schools, and benevolent societies. Black people associated with these institutions fought for the manumission of their less fortunate brothers and sisters, lobbied for an end to the slave trade and of the institution of slavery. They rooted their arguments in the language of natural rights and democratic principles and became the conscience of the nation. [3]

Although the rise of the free black population is one of the most notable achievements of the Revolutionary Era, it is important to note that the overall impact of the Revolution on slavery had negative consequences. In rice-growing regions of South Carolina and Georgia, the patriot victory confirmed the power of the master class. Doubts about slavery and legal modifications that occurred in the North and Upper South never took serious hold among whites in the Lower South. Even in Virginia, the move toward freeing some slaves was made more difficult by new legal restrictions in 1792. In the North, where slavery was on its way out, racism still persisted, as in a Massachusetts law of 1786 that prohibited whites from legally marrying African Americans, Indians, or people of mixed race. [5]

The Revolution clearly had a mixed impact on slavery and contradictory meanings for African Americans. [5] It failed to reconcile slavery with these new egalitarian republican societies, a tension that eventually boiled over in the 1830s and 1840s and effectively tore the nation in two in the 1850s and 1860s. [2]

Slavery and the Constitution

In the summer of 1787, political leaders of the United States met in Philadelphia to debate the creation of a new federal constitution to replace the Articles of Confederation. The Articles of Confederation reflected the ideals of the revolutionary generation who distrusted concentrated power and wanted to create a new nation that in no way resembled the monarchy they fought to overthrow. Ten years after America declared its independence from Britain, the intractable problems and glaring weaknesses of the Articles of Confederation were on full display. Rather than a strong union, the United States of America resembled thirteen separate countries each concerned about its own sovereignty and well-being rather than that of the nation. Now that the Revolutionary War was over, what common cause and purpose held the states together? The nation, it seemed, was fraying apart at the seams, threatening to splinter into a series of regional confederacies rather than a united nation.

The ardent nationalists, such as Virginia's James Madison, met in Philadelphia in 1787 to propose a new federal constitution they hoped would create "a more perfect union." They also had an opportunity to address the issue of slavery directly and, perhaps, set it on a path toward extinction since it clearly violated the principles of the American Revolution. Instead, the framers of the Constitution swept the problem of slavery under the rug with a series of compromises demanded by representatives from southern states in exchange for their support of the new constitution. These compromises ensured the constitutional protection of slavery while also setting the stage for future divisive debates over slavery that would threaten to break the union apart along sectional lines.

Of all the compromises that formed the Constitution, perhaps none would be more important than the compromise over the slave trade. Americans generally perceived the trans-Atlantic slave trade as more violent and immoral than slavery itself. Many Northerners opposed it on moral grounds. But they also understood that letting southern states import more Africans

would increase their political power. The Constitution counted each black individual as three-fifths of a person for purposes of representation, so in districts with many slaves, the white voters had extra influence.

On the other hand, the states of the Upper South also welcomed a ban on the Atlantic trade because they already had a surplus of slaves. Banning importation meant slave owners in Virginia and Maryland could get higher prices when they sold their slaves to states like South Carolina and Georgia that were dependent upon a continued slave trade.

New England and the Deep South agreed to what was called a "dirty compromise" at the Constitutional Convention in 1787. New Englanders agreed to include a constitutional provision that protected the foreign slave trade for twenty years; in exchange, South Carolina and Georgia delegates had agreed to support a constitutional clause that made it easier for Congress to pass commercial legislation. As a result, the Atlantic slave trade resumed until 1808 when it was outlawed for three reasons. First, Britain was also in the process of outlawing the slave trade in 1807, and the United States did not want to concede any moral high ground to its rival. Second, the Haitian Revolution (1791–1804), a successful slave revolt against French colonial rule in the West Indies, had changed the stakes in the debate. The image of thousands of armed black revolutionaries terrified white Americans. Third, the Haitian Revolution had ended France's plans to expand its presence in the Americas, so in 1803, the United States had purchased the Louisiana Territory from the French at a fire-sale price. This massive new territory, which had doubled the size of the United States, had put the question of slavery's expansion at the top of the national agenda. Many white Americans, including President Thomas Jefferson, thought that ending the external slave trade and dispersing the domestic slave population would keep the United States a white man's republic and perhaps even lead to the disappearance of slavery.

The ban on the slave trade, however, lacked effective enforcement measures and funding. Moreover, instead of freeing illegally imported Africans, the act left their fate to the individual states, and many of those states simply sold intercepted slaves at auction. Thus, the ban preserved the logic of property ownership in human beings. The new federal government protected slavery as much as it expanded democratic rights and privileges for white men. [2]

Conclusion

The Revolution brought change for some black people, although nothing approaching full equality. The courageous military service of African Americans and the revolutionary spirit ended slavery in New England almost immediately. The middle states of New York, Pennsylvania, and New Jersey adopted policies of gradual emancipation from 1780 to 1804. Many of the founders opposed slavery in principle (including some whose wealth was largely in human property). Individual manumissions increased following the Revolution.

Still, free blacks in both the North and South faced persistent discrimination in virtually every aspect of life, notably employment, housing, and education. Many of the founders hoped that slavery would eventually disappear in the American South. When cotton became king in the South after 1800, this hope died. There was just too much profit to be made working slaves on cotton plantations. The statement of human equality in the Declaration of Independence was never entirely forgotten, however. It remained as an ideal that could be appealed to by abolitionists and civil rights activists through the following decades. [5]

4.5: Primary Sources

Primary Source Document: Petition of Slaves in Boston, Province of Massachusetts Bay by Felix
Document Download Link

Primary Source Document: Freedom Petition of Prince Hall
Document Download Link

Public domain content

- Felix (Unknown) Slave Petition for Freedom (January 6. 1773) . **Authored by**: Lover of constitutional liberty. **Located at**: https://archive.org/details/appendixorsomeob00love/page/8. **Project**: The Appendix: or Some observations on the expediency of the petition of the Africans living in Boston. **License**: *Public Domain: No Known Copyright*
- Petition for freedom to the Massachusetts Council and the House of Representatives, January 1777u00a0. **Provided by**: Massachusetts Historical Society. **Located at**: https://www.masshist.org/database/557. **License**: *Public Domain: No Known Copyright*

CHAPTER OVERVIEW

5: CREATING AN AFRICAN-AMERICAN CULTURE

5.1: Introduction

Creating an African-American Culture

Module Introduction

People express cultural meaning through their language, food, sacred and secular rites, ceremonies, rituals, art, music, dance, personal adornment, celebrations and many other socio-cultural customs and practices. [3]

Despite slavery's strictures, African Americans created their own unique culture and cultural identity, particularly through language and religion, during the eighteenth and nineteenth century.

This module explores how black people created an African American culture and identity, how they used language, literacy, religion, and music, such as spirituals, hymns, and hollers, to navigate and resist a dehumanizing slave system and strengthen the bonds of their communities. [1]

Learning Outcomes

This module addresses the following Course Learning Outcomes listed in the Syllabus for this course:

- To provide students with a general understanding of the history of African Americans within the context of American History.
- To motivate students to become interested and active in African American history by comparing current events with historical information.[1]

Additional learning outcomes associated with this module are:

- The student will be able to discuss the origins, evolution, and spread of racial slavery.
- The student will be able to describe the creation of a distinct African-American culture and how that culture became part of the broader American culture. [1]

Module Objectives

Upon completion of this module, the student will be able to:

- Discuss the role of language and religion as they relate to the creation of a unique African American culture.
- Analyze the roles of language and religion in shaping cultural identities in America today. [1]

Readings and Resources

Learning Unit: Creating an African-American Culture: Language, Religion, and Music (see below) [1]

CC licensed content, Original

- **Authored by**: Florida State College at Jacksonville. **License**: *CC BY: Attribution*

Public domain content

- Park Ethnography Program. **Provided by**: National Park Service. **Located at**: https://www.nps.gov/ethnography/aah/aaheritage/histContextsA.htm. **Project**: African American Heritage and Ethnography. **License**: *Public Domain: No Known Copyright*

5.2: Language

Creating an African-American Culture—Language, Religion, and Music

Language

For the first generations of Africans enslaved in the colonies, language accommodation and acculturation were a necessity for their survival in the Western world. Depending upon when and where they came from in Africa, in addition to their own languages, different African people had varying degrees of language competence in English, Spanish, Portuguese and Dutch. As a result of trade with the Portuguese in the middle fifteenth century, bilingualism arose among West Africans along the coast. In succeeding centuries, as West Africans traded with the Dutch, French and English, some Africans continued to at least understand, and many to speak, some form of one or more European languages. Even though they spoke many different African languages, many Africans who had participated in long distance trading on the African continent spoke a "lingua franca" or trade language that allowed them to communicate among themselves (Abrahams 1983:26). African sailors on European vessels may have also spoken a "maritime jargon" (Berlin 1998; Birmingham 1981; McWhorter 1997, 2000a). The first generations of Africans and Europeans who came into contact with one another, like all people of different language groups, spoke their own language and developed a pidgin , language. Pidgins included words and meaning from both languages that allowed them to communicate.

Over time, both Africans and Europeans communicated in some form of creole . People of Angola and West Central Africa developed *Angolar Creole Portuguese* , a language still spoken by descendants of maroon slaves who escaped from Portuguese plantations on São Tomé beginning in the middle sixteenth century. People who were enslaved by the Spanish developed Spanish-based creoles, called *Papiamentu Creole Spanish :Palenquero* is another Spanish creole developed by Africans in maroon settlements of what is now Colombia, South America. Enslaved Africans in New Netherlands, later New York, developed a Dutch-based creole, *Negerhollands Creole Dutch* , in Haiti and later in Louisiana people spoke a French-based creole, today called *Haitian Creole French* . In the English colonies Africans spoke an English-based *Atlantic Creole* , generally called plantation creole. Lowcountry Africans spoke an English-based creole that came to be called *Gullah* . *Gullah* is a language closely related to *Krio* a creole spoken in Sierra Leone. [3]

Enslaved African American Language

Gullah and other creoles emerged because enslaved Africans greatly outnumbered whites on colonial plantations as occurred in the Lowcountry, especially on the sea islands where *Gullah* developed. John McWhorter, a linguist, advances an " *Afrogenesis Theory* " of creole origins, stressing the importation of most plantation creoles from West African trade settlements. There creole languages originated in interactions between white traders and slaves, some of whom were eventually transported overseas (McWhorter 2000a, 2000b). The *Afrogenesis Theory* helps explain why *Gullah* and *Krio* are similar creoles.

Historian Lorena Walsh notes that, " *Gullah* ," attained creole status during the first decades of the 1700s, and was learned and used by the second generation of slaves as their mother tongue. Around the same time, in the 1720 and 1730s, Anglican clergy were still reporting that Africans spoke little or no English but stood around in groups talking among themselves in "strange languages (Walsh 1997:96–97)."

In the past, enslaved Africans from Jacksonville, North Carolina to Jacksonville, Florida along the coast and 100 miles inland spoke *Gullah* . In the present, many of the descendants of the early *Gullah* speakers continue to speak a form of the language (Hancock 1992:70–72; Geraty 1997). African American heritage preservation efforts in the sea islands include attempts to maintain *Gullah* as a living language.

Runaway advertisements noted enslaved people's distinctive language characteristics and level of language proficiency as identifiers. A search of runaway advertisements 1736–1776 in the Virginia Gazette, Williamsburg, Virginia yielded advertisements for five men described as "Angola negroes" or born in Angola. Two could speak very good English, two " speak English tolerably good " and one was described as stammering. Two advertisements identified "Eboe negroe." One could "speak tolerable good English." Jemmy, John and Boston in this image illustrate the range of English language competency among African-born men in eighteenth century Virginia.

As part of a more extensive study of comments on language found in runaways advertisements in eight colonies and, later, states, historian Michael Gomez examined the quality of English spoken by 99 Africans in Virginia from 1736 to 1836. He found that the advertisement's descriptions said 39 Africans spoke "none, little or very little, 36 spoke "bad," "very bad" or "broken" English and 24 spoke "good" or very good" English (1998:177–180).

> prevent all masters of ships from carrying him off, as who-
> ever conveys him away may expect to be prosecuted accor-
> ding to law by   HUGH WYLIE.
>
> _____
>
> NORFOLK, *Jan.* 3, 1770.
>
> RUN away from the subscriber, the
> 13th of *November* last, a Negro fellow named
> BRISTOL, about 5 feet 8 inches high, very black,
> thick lipped, has lost some of his fore teeth, marked
> with the small-pox, and speaks good *English,* some
> *French* and *Spanish.* He was seen last month at *Rich-*
> *mond,* calling himself *Tom,* passing for a freeman, and
> may go out of the country as such. Any person who will
> secure him, so that I can get him, shall be paid Forty
> Shillings more than the law allows ; and all masters of
> vessels are forewarned from carrying him out of the
> country, as he may impose on them by saying he is free
> if.   MAXIMILIAN CALVERT.
>
> TAKEN up on *Crooked Run,* in *Lunenburg* county.

Figure 5-1: Virginia Gazette (Rind), Williamsburg, November 30, 1769 by Virginia Gazette is in the Public Domain .An advertisement published by a subscriber looking for one of his runaway slaves named Bristol.

According to Gomez, those African runaways 30 years of age or older or who had been in North America more than 3 years were most likely to speak good English. Like the Virginia Africans, over 70 percent of Africans running away from South Carolina, Georgia were also described as speaking "bad, very bad, very little, or no English." Among Louisiana runaways, they were about equally divided between those who could speak French and those that could not. Gomez found the few women in the study were slightly more likely than the men to speak French or English (1998:179).

Many enslaved people were multi-lingual. "Without a doubt," historian Philip Morgan contends, "blacks were the most linguistically polyglot and proficient ethnic group in the Americas (2002:139)."

The continuous arrival of new African slaves influenced the language spoken by American-born Africans in the rural colonial Chesapeake and Lowcountry regions up until 1807. Even after this date, smugglers sold Africans in the region, right up until the Civil War (Kashif 2001). In contrast, many free African Americans in the southern colonies became more acculturated in speech and literate, along with all other European cultural customs, as they consciously sought to differentiate themselves from their enslaved sisters and brothers. [3]

Public domain content

- Park Ethnography Program. **Provided by**: National Park Service. **Located at**: https://www.nps.gov/ethnography/aah/aaheritage/histContextsA.htm. **Project**: African American Heritage and Ethnography. **License**: *Public Domain: No Known Copyright*
- Virginia Gazette (Rind), Williamsburg, November 30, 1769. **Provided by**: Virginia Gazette. **Located at**: http://www2.vcdh.virginia.edu/gos/search/relatedAd.php?adFile=rg70.xml&adId=v1770020487. **License**: *Public Domain: No Known Copyright*

5.3: Spiritual Life- Public and Secret

Spiritual Life: Public & Secret

Along with language, black people also created a unique African American culture through religious expression and practices. By the eighteenth century, many of the people brought from West Central African to be enslaved in the Americas were familiar if not converted to Catholicism. Before the American Revolution most black Catholics lived in Maryland and in the areas that were to become Florida and Louisiana. In the American colonies controlled by Catholic powers—the Portuguese, Spanish and French—African slaves were baptized as Christians from the earliest days of slavery. But in the British-controlled Protestant colonies, planters showed little interest in converting their slaves. Many feared that to accept slaves as Christians was to acknowledge that "Negroes" were entitled to rights accorded other Christians—a dangerous message as far as they were concerned.

As early as 1654, the English made provisions for "negro" servants to receive religious instruction and education. Some planters made provisions in their will that their "negro servants be freed, that they should be taught to read and write, make their own clothes and be brought up in the fear of God." By 1770, it had become the duty of masters acquiring free "negro children as apprenticed to agree to teach them reading, writing and arithmetic" (Russell [1913] 1969:138).

Despite owner opposition, and the inability of some Africans to speak or understand English, by 1724 Anglican clergymen had established small groups of African converts to Protestant Christianity in a number of parishes in Virginia and Maryland. Their greatest success was in Bruton parish, Williamsburg, eight miles north of Carter's Grove, where approximately 200 Africans were baptized.

The slaves who lived at Carter's Grove apparently chose to attend Bruton Parish church over other Anglican churches located nearer to their homes and attended by the Burwell Family. Although the journey to Willamsburg was longer it was also an occasion when they could meet with friends or relatives from Bray and Kingsmill Farm or other surrounding plantations or farms (Russell [1913] 1969:138). In the last half of the eighteenth century 1,122 "negro-baptisms were recorded" in Bruton Parish by the Anglican church (Wilson 1923:49).

The motivation for attending church was as likely to be a rare chance to meet without fear of planter intervention as it was spiritual. Christians came from different generation groups and were as likely to be field hands as they were to be domestic servants in the great houses. Christians included Africans and native-born African Virginians. For some, the motivation was a reward of larger food rations or additional clothing. For others it was an opportunity to learn to read.

South Carolinian colonists were the first to make systematic efforts to Christianize enslaved Africans and African Americans in the early eighteenth century. Anglicans believed literacy was essential. As Anglican missionaries reached out to enslaved Africans in South Carolina and Georgia they tried to teach at least a few to read. Planters were hostile to the idea of slave literacy. They resisted by passing a law in 1734 that slaves could not leave the plantation on "Sundays, fast days, and holy days without a ticket," that is a pass. Fears of insurrections led by literate slaves, such as the Stono Rebellion in South Carolina, resulted in passage of the New Negro Act of 1740, which curtailed the missionaries' freedom to teach slaves to read and write English. In spite of the law, Alexander Garden, an Anglican missionary, established the Charleston Negro School in 1743. The school lasted twenty years. Garden purchased and taught two African American boys to read and write and they became teachers of others. Over the next four years Garden graduated forty "scholars." At its peak in 1755, the school enrolled seventy African American children. This was a miniscule number considering there were about 50,000 Africans and African Americans in the colony. It was, however, a start (Frey 1991:20–24).

Figure 5-2: DE Unitas Fractum Bild 04 by David Cranz is in the Public Domain .A 1757 drawing titled, "Exorcism-Baptism of the Negroes," that shows African American slaves being baptized in a Moravian Church in North Carolina.

Other Protestant sects also reached out to African slaves in southern colonies. The Presbyterians established a church on Edisto Island, South Carolina between 1710 and 1720. Thirty years later, Moravians, mostly missionaries to American Indians, established a North Carolina church that received African slaves into the congregation.

During the first Great Awakening of the 1740s, itinerant Baptist and Methodist preachers spread the Gospel into slave communities. The Baptists and Methodists did not insist on a well-educated clergy. They believed true preachers were called and anointed by the spirit of God, not groomed in institutions of higher learning. If a converted slave demonstrated a call to preach, he could potentially preach to both black and white audiences. Consequently, African American slaves tended to most often join or attend Baptist and Methodist churches. (Raboteau 1978:133–134; Creel 1988; 78–80). [3] The first independent African American churches that slaves established in the 1770s were a part of the Baptist denomination: Silver Bluff Baptist Church in South Carolina, First Baptist Church of Petersburg, Virginia, and First African Baptist Church of Savannah, Georgia. [1]

FAMILY WORSHIP IN A PLANTATION IN SOUTH CAROLINA.—SEE PAGE 574

Family Worship in a Plantation in South Carolina (page 561) by unknown is in the Public Domain .From *The Illustrated London News* , December 5, 1863, p. 561.

A recording of a prayer from a Baptist church in Livingston, Alabama (1939)

An audio element has been excluded from this version of the text. You can listen to it online here: pb.libretexts.org/aa/?p=78

Prayer by John A. Lomax (Collector) has no known copyright restrictions. [8]

(Transcript)

Additional link to audio.

Public and Secret Religious Experience

The first Great Awakening accelerated the spread of Christianity and a Christian culture among African Americans. The Presbyterians launched the first sporadic revivals in the 1740s. Baptist revivals began in the 1760s followed ten years later by the Methodists. With religious conversion came education for the enslaved, at least education to read the Bible. By 1771, itinerant African American Baptist preachers were conducting services, sometimes secretly, in and around Williamsburg, Virginia.

Aside from the names of a small number of runaway slaves who were described as fond of preaching or singing hymns, many of the early African American preachers remain anonymous. The few names in the historical record were men of uncommon accomplishments in organizing churches, church schools, and mutual aid societies in the South and as missionaries in Jamaica and Nova Scotia. All were born into slavery in Virginia. All were Baptists. George Liele, born in 1737 was the first African American ordained as a Baptist minister. He preached to whites and slaves on the indigo and rice plantations along the Savannah River in Georgia. He was freed during the Revolutionary War in the will of his owner. Liele was forced to flee with

the British to Jamaica in order to escape re-enslavement by his owner's heirs. Before he left, he baptized several converts, including Reverend Andrew Bryan, who would continue his work in Georgia and as missionaries extend it abroad.

"Our brother Andrew was one of the black hearers of George Liele, … prior to the departure of George Liele for Jamaica, he came up the Tybee River … and baptized our brother Andrew, with a wench of the name of Hagar, both belonging to Jonathon Bryan, Esq.; these were the last performances of our Brother George Liele in this quarter, About eight or nine months after his departure, Andrew began to exhort his black hearers, with a few whites… (Letters showing the Rise of Early Negro Churches 1916:77–78)

Liele also baptized David George, a Virginia runaway. These men, and others, formed the nucleus of slaves who were organized by a white preacher as the Silver Bluff Baptist Church between 1773 and 1775. George began to preach during the Revolutionary War, but later fled with the British to Nova Scotia where he established the second Baptist church in the province (Frey 1991:37–39).

In 1782, Andrew Bryan organized a church in Savannah that was certified in the Baptist Annual Register in 1788 as follows:

"This is to certify, that upon examination into the experiences and characters of a number of Ethiopians, and adjacent to Savannah it appears God has brought them out of darkness into the light of the gospel… This is to certify, that the Ethiopian church of Jesus Christ, have called their beloved Andrew to the work of the ministry…." (Letters showing the Rise of Early Negro Churches 1916:78).

As the eighteenth century ended, the First African Baptist Church in Savannah erected its first building. By 1800, Bryan's congregation had grown to about 700, leading to a reorganization that created the First Baptist Church of Savannah. Fifty of Bryan's adult members could read, having been taught the Bible and the Baptist Confession of Faith. First African Baptist established the first black led Sunday school for African Americans, and Henry Francis, who had been ordained by Bryan, operated a school for Georgia's black children. [3]

Cultural Resistance: "Gimmee" That Old Time Religion!

Not all Africans and African Americans embraced Christianity, however. Some resisted by retaining their native African spiritual practices or their Islamic faith. Historians point out that a number of Africans who arrived in America were Muslims and that they never relinquished their faith in Islam.

There is relatively little historical documentation on eighteenth century enslaved Muslims in North America making discussion of them less conclusive than that about enslaved Africans who were Christians or who practiced indigenous traditional African religions. Some scholars believe that perhaps as many as 10% of Africans enslaved in North America between 1711 and 1715 were Muslims and that the majority probably were literate (Deeb 2002).

Islam was firmly established as a religion in Ancient Mali as early as the fourteenth century. As in other parts of the world, Islamic conversion occurred through trade and migration far more often than by force. In West Africa, prior to the eighteenth century, much of this conversion occurred through interaction of West Africans with Berber traders who controlled the trans-Saharan trade routes. From the early seventeenth century through the late eighteenth century, the influence of Islam spread among the people in many parts of the Senegambia region, the interior of Sierra Leone, the Gold Coast and as far south as the Bight of Benin.

According to historian Michael Gomez, the widespread influence of Islam in West Africa makes it highly likely that the numbers of Muslim Africans enslaved was probably in the thousands (1998:86). The recurrence of Muslim names among American-born Africans running away from enslavement in eighteenth century South Carolina offers some evidence of Muslim people's presence and their efforts to continue their faith (Gomez 1998:60).

Historian Sylviane A. Diouf estimates at least 100,000 Africans brought to the Americas were Muslims, including political and religious leaders, traders, students, Islamic scholars, and judges. In some cases, these enslaved African Muslims were more educated than their American masters. According to Diouf, the captivity of several of the notable Muslim slaves who left narratives of their experiences grew out of complex religious, political, and social conflicts in West Africa after the disintegration of the Wolof Empire. Diouf argues, the religious principles and practices of African Muslims, including their literacy, made them resistant to enslavement and promoted their social differentiation from other enslaved Africans. As slaves, they were prohibited from reading and writing and had no ink or paper. Instead they used wood tablets and organic plant juices or stones to write with. Some wrote, in Arabic, verses of the Koran they knew by heart, so as not to forget how to write.

According to Diouf, Arabic was used by slaves to plot revolts in Guyana, Rio de Janeiro and Santo Domingo because the language was not understood by slave owners. Manuscripts in Arabic of maps and blueprints for revolts also have been found in North America, Jamaica and Trinidad (Diouf 1998).

Diouf contends many enslaved Muslims went to great efforts to preserve the pillars of Islamic ritual because it allowed them "to impose a discipline on themselves rather than to submit to another people's discipline" (1998:162). Diouf identifies references in the historical literature of slavery to the persistence of Islamic cultural practices among enslaved Muslims such as the wearing of turbans, beards, and protective rings; the use of prayer mats, beads, and talismans (*gris-gris*); and the persistence of Islamic dietary customs. For Diouf, *saraka* cakes cooked on Sapelo Island in Georgia were probably associated with *sadakha* or meritorious alms offered in the name of Allah. She speculates that the circular ring shout performed in Sea Island praise or prayer houses might have been a recreation of the Muslim custom of circumambulation of the Kaaba during the pilgrimage in Mecca. Arabic literacy, according to Diouf, generated powers of resistance because it served as a resource for spiritual inspiration and communal organization, "A tradition of defiance and rebellion (1998:145)."

Priests of African traditional religions also often continued to hold their beliefs. Even though over time the majority of Africans and African Americans became Christians, African Christianity and church rituals often incorporated African beliefs and rituals. Some scholars suggest that Africans readily acculturated to Christianity, especially those from West Central Africa, because of prior exposure to Christianity. Old ways died hard and some never died out. Historian John Thornton points out that none of the Christian movements in the Kongo brought about a radical break with Kongo religious or ideological past. Instead African Christianity simply emphasized already active tendencies in the worldview of the Kongo people (Thornton 1983:62–63).

Figure 5-4: Kongo Crucifix by Cliff1066 is licensed under CC BY 2.0 .Image of a seventeenth century crucifix made by Portuguese missionaries that combines the Kongo custom of using scepters and staffs as emblems of power with the representation of Christ as an African.

One of the central beliefs of the Kongo, for example, emphasizes that human beings move through existence in counterclockwise circularity like the movement of the sun, coming into life or waking up in the east, grow to maturity reaching the height of their powers in the north, die and pass out of life in the west into life after death in the south then come back in

the east being born again (Fu-Kiah 1969; Thompson 1984; McGaffey 1986). Many West African groups believe in life after death and some believes that people are reborn in their descendants. These ideas, although in a different context, blended well with Christian beliefs in life after death and with the Christian belief being born again. [3]

5.4: Performing Culture in Music and Dance

Performing Culture in Music & Dance

Not only did African Americans often blend traditional West African spirituality with Christian beliefs, they also wove together West African rhythms, shouts, and melodies with European American tunes to create spiritual songs drawn from images and stories found in Bible. African Americans also put their own unique cultural and musical stamp on a style of hymn singing called lined-out hymnody. Lined-out hymn singing has roots in sixteenth and seventeenth century England and Scotland. Baptist, Methodist, and Presbyterian missionaries taught lining out to slaves and poor whites in the South where literacy was low and hymnbooks were few. Taken together, African American spirituals and hymns represent a profound cultural expression and contribution that laid the foundation for future forms of American music including the blues, soul, jazz, and even rock n' roll and hip-hop.

African American spiritual songs took a variety of forms including shouts, anthems, and jubilees. "Styles ranged from the exciting tempo and rhythmic stamp of the shout to the slow, drawn-out 'sorrow songs' which usually come to mind when the spirituals are mentioned," observes historian Albert J. Raboteau. "While the lyrics and themes of the spirituals were drawn from Biblical verses and Christian hymns, and although the music and melodies were strongly influenced by the sacred and secular songs of white Americans, the style in which the slaves sang the spirituals was African." (Raboteau, 74). The influence of West Africa could be heard in the spirituals' call-and-response form, syncopated rhythms, and the use of "blue" notes, which are tones in the major and pentatonic scale that are "bent" into minor tones. African Americans also demonstrated their West African heritage in their body movements, including hand-clapping, foot-stomping, and dance. (Darden, 2004) [1]

The Ring Shout

The heritage of West Africa found perhaps its fullest expression in the spiritual form called the ring shout, which seemed to thrive on the sea islands of South Carolina, Georgia, and Florida. The ring shout combines singing or shouting stories from the Bible with a religious form of dance that resembles shuffling. In a religious setting, the shouters shuffle and stomp in a counterclockwise motion while clapping their hands to the shout's rhythm. Some African American slaves believed the ring shout was a central part of worship, often a prerequisite to receiving the spirit or having a conversion experience. The ring shout, argues Raboteau, was thus a "two-way bridge connecting the core of West African religions—possession by the gods—to the core of evangelical Protestantism—experience of conversion." (Raboteau, 73)

During the Civil War, William Francis Allen, a northern educator, heard the religious singing of newly freed slaves while in the Low Country of South Carolina. He later helped edit and publish the first collection of African American religious songs in American history, *Slave Songs of the United States* . In an 1867 article in *The Nation* , Allen described the ring shout in the following manner:

"…the true 'shout' takes place on Sundays or on 'praise' nights through the week, and either in the praise-house or in some cabin in which a regular religious meeting has been held… The benches are pushed back to the wall when the meeting is over, and old and young men and women… boys… young girls barefooted, all stand up in the middle of the floor, and when the [spiritual] is struck, begin first walking and by-and-by shuffling round, one after the other, in a ring. The foot is hardly taken from the floor, and the progression is mainly due to a jerking, hitching motion, which agitates the entire shouter, and soon brings out streams of perspiration. Sometimes they dance silently, sometimes as they shuffle they sing the chorus of the spiritual, and sometimes they song itself is also sung by the dancers…. Song and dance alike are extremely energetic, and often, when the shout lasts into the middle of the night, the monotonous thud, thud, thud of feet prevents sleep within half a mile of the praise-house… It is not unlikely that this remarkable religious ceremony is a relic of some African dance…" (Allen quoted in Rabotaeu, 71)

During the 1930s, the folklorists Alan and John Lomax, found evidence of the ring shout still practiced in Louisiana, Texas, Georgia, and the Bahamas, and versions of it in Haiti. (Rabotaeu, 1978, 70) The ring shout is still performed today by the descendants of slaves, particularly in McIntosh County, Georgia. Versions of the ring shout can also be seen today in some African American Primitive Baptist churches in Georgia and Florida. Congregants often sing spirituals during the offering portion of the service and some will move toward the front of church and "rock" counter-clockwise around the communion table while singing old spirituals like "Climbing Jacob's Ladder." [1]

Lined-Out Hymns

As Baptist, Methodist, and Presbyterian missionaries spread the gospel during the eighteenth and nineteenth century, including into African American slave communities, they brought with them hymns composed by English hymn writers such as Issac Watts, William Cowper, and Charles Wesley. In many poor white and slave communities, church attendees could not read or afford hymnbooks. As a result, missionaries taught church congregations the practice of lining out hymns. Lining out involved a preacher or deacon standing before a congregation and reading the first lines of a hymn from a hymnbook or speaking them from memory. The congregation, which most likely did not have hymnbooks or were usually unable to read them if they did, would hear the lines intoned by the presenter and then respond by singing them, often very slowly, to a familiar tune that fit the hymn's meter. The practice of lining out originated in England following the Protestant Reformation and spread to Scotland and then North America where the Puritans lined out the Psalms from their Bay Psalm Book. Lining out quickly took hold among white and black Baptists in particular during the eighteenth century and nineteenth century.

One slave master, and Presbyterian missionary, from Liberty County, Georgia, Charles Colcock Jones, emphasized the importance of teaching hymns and psalms to slaves as way to dissuade them from singing the "extravagant and nonsensical chants" and shouts "of their own composing." Ironically, however, black slaves used these European hymn and psalm texts to learn literacy. And by creating their own melodies, tunes, and speech patterns when lining out the hymns, African Americans effectively "blackened" what was originally a European form of singing. African American slaves in turn created a unique African American musical sound and culture that became the bedrock of later secular genres such as the blues. (Dargan, 2006)

William Francis Allen, who described the ring shout tradition among African American slaves during the Civil War, also provided one of the most detailed and evocative descriptions of lined-out hymn singing among slaves during the same time period:

"I went to the Praise House in the Quarters.... They were just beginning a hymn, which the preacher deaconed [lined] out, two lines at a time. The tune was evidently Old Hundred, which was maintained throughout by one voice or another, but curiously varied at every note so as to form an intricate intertwining of harmonious sounds. It was something very different from anything I ever heard, and no description I have read conveys any notion of it. There were no parts properly speaking, only now and then a hint of a base or tenor, and the modulation seemed to be just the inspiration of the moment—no effort at regularity, only that one or two voices kept up the air—but the ears are so good, and the time is so perfectly kept... that there was very seldom a discordant note. It might be compared to the notes of an organ or orchestra, where all harmony is poured out in accompaniment of the air." (Allen quoted in Dargan, 112–13)

Lined-out hymns in the black church also became known as long meter hymns, metered hymns, or "Dr. Watts" because of the large number of hymns penned by Issac Watts. Until the late twentieth century, lined-out hymns were almost always sung a capella—that is with voices only and without musical accompaniment.

George Pullen Jackson, a folklorist and professor, visited black Primitive Baptist churches in Alabama and Jacksonville, Florida in the 1940s and heard congregants still singing lined-out hymns, which he sometimes called "surge songs," with great power and beauty:

"The 'long meter' hymns (absolute opposites of the spirituals in every sense) are sung in thousands of unspoiled [black] congregations usually, but not exclusively, at the opening of the service. A deacon or the elder 'lines out' a couplet of the text in a sing-song voice and at a fair speaking pace ending on definite tone. This 'tones' the tune. The deacon then starts singing, and by the time he has sung through the elaborately ornamented first syllable the whole congregation has joined in on the second syllable with a volume of florid sound which ebbs and flows slowly, powerfully and at times majestically in successive surges until the lined-out words have been sung.... No instrument is ever used." (Jackson, 248)

The lined-out hymn singing tradition still thrives in some black churches, particularly in Missionary and Primitive Baptist congregations. Black Primitive Baptists maintain the strongest tradition, however. They sing numerous hymns from their hymnbook, The Primitive Hymns, which contains only texts and no musical notations, during all parts of their church services. The Primitive Baptists also draw from the deepest well of hymn tunes, which have been passed down orally over many generations. Primitive Baptist associations in states such as Alabama, Florida, Georgia, North Carolina, and Virginia also have their own unique hymn tunes and rhythms while sharing the same hymn texts and manner of lining out. [1]

Below are two examples of lined-out hymns:

An audio element has been excluded from this version of the text. You can listen to it online here: pb.libretexts.org/aa/?p=80

Go Preach My Gospel by John A. Lomax (Collector) has no know copyright restrictions. [9]

Additional link to audio.

Lyrics:

"Go preach my gospel," saith the Lord, "Bid the whole earth my grace receive, Explain to them my sacred word, Bid them believe, obey, and live." "I'll make my great commission known, And ye shall prove my gospel true.

An audio element has been excluded from this version of the text. You can listen to it online here: pb.libretexts.org/aa/?p=80

Jesus, My God, I Know His Name by John A. Lomax (Collector) has no know copyright restrictions. [10]

Additional link to audio.

Lyrics:

Jesus, my God I know his name His name is on my soul He will not put my soul to shamebr Oh let my holy Lord)

Black Secular Music

African Americans also created their own body of secular songs during the trials of slavery. These included work songs and hollers as well as drum rhythms and songs composed on stringed instruments like banjos. Work songs helped to ease the drudgery of plantation labor while hollers resembled laments that provided emotional release or allowed slaves to communicate covert messages that might spread from plantation to plantation. These songs showed the individual and collective creativity of black people and their desire to create and maintain a sense of community and resist the dehumanizing and destructive forces of slavery. [1]

One example of how black people used music to create a sense of community is from Charleston, South Carolina where African Americans would travel to rural areas to participate in countryside dances where they danced all night. Slaves continued to hold countryside dances at night throughout the eighteenth century, even after the Stono Rebellion in 1730 when slave dances were outlawed along with use or ownership of drums, horns and other loud instruments (Morgan 1998:580–582).

Enslaved African Americans communicated with one another in hollers or calls derived from their musical tradition of call and response. *Calls* are as musical ways "to communicate messages of all kinds-to bring people in from the fields, to summon them to work, to attract the attention of a girl in the distance, to signal hunting dogs, or simply to make one's presence known Courlander 1963:81)." *Calls* convey simple messages, or merely make one's whereabouts known to friends working elsewhere in the fields. Many slave calls were modeled on African drumming. Slaves also copied the drum rhythms by 'patting juba.' This procedure involved "foot tapping, hand clapping, and thigh slapping, all in precise rhythm (Southern 1971:168)." Patting juba was incorporated into an early twentieth century dance called the Charleston. This "Africanism," reappeared in the late twentieth century in the dance choreography of the Broadway musical "Bring on the Noise, Bring on the Funk."

Figure 5-5: Slave dance to banjo by Anonymous is in the Public Domain .The Old Plantation (anonymous folk painting late 1700s). Depicts African-American slaves dancing to banjo and percussion

African Americans also made and played banjos made out of gourds. The banjo is a musical instrument that originated in Senegal and the Gambia region of West Africa. By the end of the eighteenth century banjos had become the most common musical accompaniment used by Africans for their dances. The first mention of it in North America is found in a 1749 account of a Christmas celebration of Africans from plantations along the Cooper River playing the banjo, dancing and making merry (Ravitz 1960:384; Coolen 1984:117–132). This famous watercolor painting *The Old Plantation* which portrays a slave dance in eighteenth century South Carolina illustrates one slave playing a banjo and another beating a drum. The musical instruments and styles of dress reveal the intertwining of influences from African and Europe.

Enslaved Africans learned to play European instruments as well. "A black Virginia born Negro fellow named Sambo," who ran away in 1766, was a carpenter who made fiddles and played them. Gabriel, a weaver by trade…is fond of reading and plays well the violin," so said his owner in a 1776 newspaper advertisement seeking his capture and return. A number of these advertisements for runaway musicians also note that they could read and some could write well enough to have possibly forged a pass. Other runaways were drawn to a different kind of cultural performance in the Christian church. Jemmy, a dark mulatto man was fond of singing hymns, Jupiter alias Gibb was a "great New Light preacher." Charles, a sawyer and shoemaker by trade also "reads tolerable well, and is a great preacher, from which I…[his owner]…imagine he will endeavour [sic] to pass for a freeman (Virginia Runaways, 2004; Jupiter, October 1, 1767; Charles, October 27, 1765; Jemmy, September 8, 1775)." [3]

Conclusion

The creation of a unique African American culture through language and religion not only allowed black people to resist the brutality of slavery and create a cohesive sense of community, it also helped spark an abolitionist movement in America. In the second half of the eighteenth century, following the spread of evangelical Christianity during and after the Great Awakening, runaway slaves, such as Jemmy, Gibb, and Charles, embodied important characteristics of a new African American culture, including religion and music, and, it seems, drew from them the inspiration and courage to flee bondage for freedom.

In the nineteenth century, black abolitionists, including David Walker, Frederick Doulgass, Nat Turner, and Sojourner Truth, used their literacy, language and religion to make forceful pleas for the humanity of black people and the immediate end of slavery. They became the vanguard of the most radical abolitionist movement in American history. [1]

CC licensed content, Original

- **Authored by**: Florida State College at Jacksonville. **License**: *CC BY: Attribution*

Public domain content

- Park Ethnography Program. **Provided by**: National Park Service. **Located at**: https://www.nps.gov/ethnography/aah/aaheritage/histContextsA.htm. **Project**: African American Heritage and Ethnography. **License**: *Public Domain: No Known Copyright*
- Slave dance to banjo. **Located at**: commons.wikimedia.org/wiki/File:Slave_dance_to_banjo,_1780s.jpg. **License**: *Public Domain: No Known Copyright*
- Go Preach My Gospel. **Authored by**: John A. Lomax (Collector). **Located at**: https://www.loc.gov/item/lomaxbib000532/. **License**: *Public Domain: No Known Copyright*
- Jesus, My God, I Know His Name. **Authored by**: John A. Lomax (Collector). **Located at**: https://www.loc.gov/item/lomaxbib000324/. **License**: *Public Domain: No Known Copyright*

CHAPTER OVERVIEW

6: THE ABOLITIONIST MOVEMENT

6.1: Introduction

The Abolitionist Movement

Module Introduction

During the first half of the nineteenth-century, a vocal if marginalized abolitionist movement developed in the United States. It was a diverse and occasionally fractious movement. Slaves fought for their freedom, and the end of slavery, by organizing and leading rebellions or running away to freedom in the North or Canada. Some of those former slaves, like Frederick Douglass, became leaders in the abolitionist movement by the force of their oratory and writing.

The transatlantic religious revivals of the early nineteenth-century, often referred to as the Second Great Awakening in the United States, inspired others, including some white men and women, to become abolitionists. They saw slavery as a grave American sin that the nation must purge to redeem itself and to prepare the way for Christ's return and 1,000-year rule on Earth. Rather than just relying on natural rights arguments, nineteenth-century abolitionists often used moral arguments – moral suasion – to highlight the immorality of slavery. In keeping with the religious fervor of the era, abolitionists hoped to bring about a mass conversion in public opinion to end slavery. Nevertheless, the vast majority of white Americans, even in the North, saw abolitionism as a radical, irrational, and dangerous threat, not only to slavery but to white supremacy and the union.

Though abolition would only come about because of the Civil War, the abolitionist movement left behind a revolutionary legacy. It used new means of communication, including mass printing presses, and new forms of literature in America, such as the slave narrative and novel, to organize its movement and spread ideas that indelibly changed the nation and the world. [1]

Learning Outcomes

This module addresses the following Course Learning Outcomes listed in the Syllabus for this course:

- To provide students with a general understanding of the history of African Americans within the context of American History.
- To motivate students to become interested and active in African American history by comparing current events with historical information.[1]

Additional learning outcomes associated with this module are:

- The student will be able to discuss the origins, evolution, and spread of racial slavery.
- The student will be able to describe the creation of a distinct African-American culture and how that culture became part of the broader American culture. [1]

Module Objectives

Upon completion of this module, the student will be able to:

Use primary historical resources to analyze the Abolitionist Movement. [1]

Readings and Resources

- Learning Unit: The Abolitionist Movement (see below) [1]
- Primary Source Documents (see below)
  - David Walker's Appeal to the Colored Citizens of the World, 1829
  - William Lloyd Garrison Introduces *The Liberator*

CC licensed content, Original

- **Authored by**: Florida State College at Jacksonville. **License**: *CC BY: Attribution*

6.2: The Abolitionist Movement

The Abolitionist Movement

Slave Uprisings

Abolitionism in North America began when enslaved Africans ran away from their masters or organized rebellions in name of freedom. Well before a religiously motivated, transatlantic, and interracial abolitionist movement developed in the nineteenth-century, numerous slave rebellions and insurrections occurred during the preceding centuries. Rebellions were rooted in the exploitative conditions of the Southern slave system. There is evidence of more than 250 uprisings or attempted uprisings, each involving 10 or more slaves from the seventeenth-century up to the Civil War.

One of the largest slave rebellions in U.S. history took place in 1811. The German Coast Uprising took place outside of New Orleans, Louisiana, and involved some 500 slaves, according to accounts; however, it only was responsible for the casualties of two white men. Volunteer militias and a detachment of the U.S. Army suppressed the rebellion. Ninety-five black people were killed as a result of executions and direct confrontations with opposing militia forces. In the weeks following the uprising, an additional forty-four accused insurgents were captured, tried, and executed.[12]

Nat Turner's Rebellion

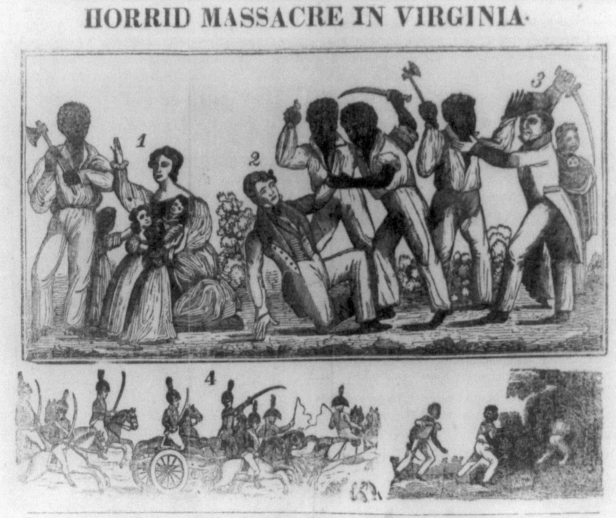

*Wood-cut depiction of the various stages of Nat Turner's Rebellion from the first massacres to the search and capture of Turner's conspirators.*Figure 6-1: Horrid Massacre in Virginia by Library of Congress has no known copyright restriction.

Another large slave uprising, Nat Turner's Rebellion, took place in 1831, in Southampton County, Virginia. Like many slaves, Nat Turner was inspired by the evangelical Protestant fervor sweeping the republic. He preached to fellow slaves in Southampton County, gaining a reputation among them as a prophet. He organized them for rebellion, awaiting a sign to begin, until an eclipse in August signaled that the appointed time had come.

Turner and as many as seventy other slaves killed their masters and their masters' families, murdering a total of around sixty-five people. Turner eluded capture until late October, when he was tried, hanged, and then beheaded and quartered. Virginia put to death fifty-six other slaves whom they believed to have taken part in the rebellion. White vigilantes killed two hundred more as panic swept through Virginia and the rest of the South.

Thomas R. Gray was a lawyer in Southampton, Virginia, where he visited Nat Turner in jail. He published *The Confessions of Nat Turner, the leader of the late insurrection in Southampton, Va., as fully and voluntarily made to Thomas R. Gray* in November 1831, after Turner had been executed:

"For as the blood of Christ had been shed on this earth, and had ascended to heaven for the salvation of sinners, and was now returning to earth again in the form of dew… it was plain to me that the Saviour was about to lay down the yoke he had borne for the sins of men, and the great day of judgment was at hand… And on the 12th of May, 1828, I heard a loud noise in the heavens, and the Spirit instantly appeared to me and said the Serpent was loosened, and Christ had laid down the yoke he had borne for the sins of men, and that I should take it on and fight against the Serpent, … Ques. Do you not find yourself mistaken now? Ans. Was not Christ crucified. And by signs in the heavens that it would make known to me when I should commence the great work—and on the appearance of the sign, (the eclipse of the sun last February) I should arise and prepare myself, and slay my enemies with their own weapons."

Discovery of Nat Turner.

"Discovery of Nat Turner" Figure 6-2: Nat Turner Captured by William Henry Shelton is in the Public Domain .

Nat Turner's Rebellion provoked a heated discussion in Virginia over slavery. The Virginia legislature was already in the process of revising the state constitution, and some delegates advocated for an easier manumission process. The rebellion, however, made that reform impossible. Virginia and other slave states recommitted themselves to the institution of slavery, and defenders of slavery in the South increasingly blamed northerners for provoking their slaves to rebel. [12]

One of those northerners who instilled fear among white southerners was David Walker, a free black man who, like Turner, advocated for rebellion if slavery did not immediately end. Walker was born a free in North Carolina in 1796. He moved to Boston in the 1820s, lectured on slavery, and promoted the first African American newspaper, *Freedom's Journal* . [11] In 1829, he published *An Appeal to the Colored Citizens of the World* , one of the most radical and impassioned abolitionist pleas in American history. Walker highlighted the nation's hypocrisies, including its promise of freedom and its sanctioning of slavery. He also called out some of the nation's Christians for their complicity in the system of slavery and their willingness to use and distort scripture from the Bible to sanction it. Walker also warned whites who practiced or tolerated slavery that their day of reckoning was close at hand. There is no evidence Nat Turner ever read *An Appeal to the Colored Citizens of the World* , but Walker's apocalyptic words foreshadowed Turner's looming rebellion. [1]

*Frontispiece from the 1830 edition of David Walker's Appeal*Figure 6-3: David Walker Appeal by Britannica Encyclopedia is in the Public Domain .

"I count my life not dear unto me, but I am ready to be offered at any moment. For what is the use of living, when in fact I am dead. But remember, Americans, that as miserable, wretched, degraded and abject as you have made us in preceding, and in this generation, to support you and your families, that some of you, (whites) on the continent of America, will yet curse the day that you ever were born. You want slaves, and want us for your slaves!!! My colour will yet, root some of you out of the very face of the earth!!!!!!" [13]

Walker died months after the publication of his Appeal, and debate continues to this day over the cause of his death. Many believe he was murdered. Regardless, Walker became a symbol of hope to free people in the North and a symbol of the terrors of literate, educated blacks to the slaveholders of the South. [11]

6.3: Atlantic Origins of Reform

Atlantic Origins of Reform

A broader, interracial abolitionist movement, one connected to the era's religious revivalism and reform campaigns that were designed to rid the nation of its moral sins, began to grow in the years after Walker published his *Appeal* . Like Walker, these abolitionists rejected attempts to gradually end slavery by colonizing black people in West Africa. They took a far more radical approach using moral arguments and persuasion to advocate slavery's immediate elimination. They publicized the atrocities committed under slavery and aimed to create a society characterized by equality of blacks and whites. In a world of intense religious fervor, they hoped to bring about a mass awakening in the United States of the sin of slavery, confident that they could transform the national conscience against the South's peculiar institution. [11]

The reform movements that emerged in the United States during the first half of the nineteenth century were not American inventions, however. Instead, these movements were rooted in a transatlantic world where both sides of the ocean faced similar problems and together collaborated to find similar solutions. Many of the same factors that spurred American reformers to action equally affected Europe. Reformers on both sides of the Atlantic visited and corresponded with one another. Exchanging ideas and building networks proved crucial to shared causes such as abolition.

Improvements in transportation, including the introduction of the steamboat, canals, and railroads, connected people not just across the United States, but also with other like-minded reformers in Europe. (Ironically, the same technologies also helped ensure that even after the abolition of slavery in the British Empire, the British remained heavily invested in slavery, both directly and indirectly.) Equally important, the reduction of publication costs created by new printing technologies in the 1830s allowed reformers to reach new audiences across the world.

Almost immediately after its publication in the United States, for instance, the escaped slave and abolitionist Frederick Douglass's autobiography was republished in Europe and translated into French and Dutch, galvanizing Douglass's supporters across the Atlantic.

Abolitionist and anti-slavery work had a decidedly transatlantic cast from its very beginnings. American Quakers began to question slavery as early as the late seventeenth century, and worked with British reformers in the successful campaign that ended the slave trade. Before, during, and after the Revolution, many Americans continued to admire European thinkers. Influence extended both east and west. By foregrounding questions about rights, the American Revolution helped inspire British abolitionists, who in turn offered support to their American counterparts. American antislavery activists developed close relationships with abolitionists on the other side of the Atlantic, such as Thomas Clarkson, Daniel O'Connell, and Joseph Sturge. Prominent American abolitionists such as Theodore Dwight Weld, Lucretia Mott, and William Lloyd Garrison were converted to the antislavery idea of immediatism—that is, the demand for emancipation without delay—by British abolitionists Elizabeth Heyrick and Charles Stuart.

Although Anglo-American antislavery networks reached back to the late eighteenth century, they dramatically grew in support and strength over the antebellum period, as evidenced by the General Antislavery Convention of 1840. This antislavery delegation consisted of more than 500 abolitionists, mostly coming from France, England, and the United States. All met together in England, united by their common goal of ending slavery in their time. Although abolitionism was not the largest American reform movement of the antebellum period (that honor belongs to temperance), it did foster greater cooperation among reformers in England and the United States. [2]

Antislavery and Abolitionism

The revivalist doctrines of salvation, perfectionism, and benevolence led many evangelical reformers to believe that slavery was the most God-defying of all sins and the most terrible blight on the moral virtue of the United States. While white interest in and commitment to abolition had existed for several decades, organized antislavery advocacy had been largely restricted to models of gradual emancipation (seen in several northern states following the American Revolution) and conditional emancipation (seen in colonization efforts to remove black Americans to settlements in Africa).

The colonization movement of the early nineteenth century had drawn together a broad political spectrum of Americans with its promise of gradually ending slavery in the United States by removing the free black population from North America. By the 1830s, however, a rising tide of anti-colonization sentiment among northern free black Americans and middle-class

evangelicals' flourishing commitment to social reform radicalized the movement. Baptists such as William Lloyd Garrison, Congregational revivalists like Arthur and Lewis Tappan and Theodore Dwight Weld, and radical Quakers including Lucretia Mott and John Greenleaf Whittier helped push the idea of immediate emancipation onto the center stage of northern reform agendas.

Inspired by a strategy known as "moral suasion," these young abolitionists believed they could convince slaveholders to voluntarily release their slaves by appealing to their sense of Christian conscience. [2] Moral suasion relied on dramatic narratives, often from former slaves, about the horrors of slavery, arguing that slavery destroyed families, as children were sold and taken away from their mothers and fathers. Moral suasion resonated with many women, who condemned the sexual violence against slave women and the victimization of southern white women by adulterous husbands. [11]

CC licensed content, Shared previously

6.4: William Lloyd Garrison

William Lloyd Garrison and the Abolitionist Movement in America

William Lloyd Garrison's early life and career famously illustrated this transition toward *immediatism*. As a young man immersed in the reform culture of antebellum Massachusetts, Garrison had fought slavery in the 1820s by advocating for both black colonization and gradual abolition. Fiery tracts penned by black northerners David Walker and James Forten, however, convinced Garrison that colonization was an inherently racist project and that African Americans possessed a hard-won right to the fruits of American liberty. So, in 1831, he established a newspaper called The Liberator, through which he organized and spearheaded an unprecedented interracial crusade dedicated to promoting immediate emancipation and black citizenship. [2]

The Liberator. Volume VII. 1837. Edited by William Lloyd Garrison. Published by Isaac Knapp, Cornhill, Boston, Massachusetts Figure 6-4: 1837 Liberator Cornhill Boston by William Lloyd Garrison is in the Public Domain .

In Garrison's first edition of *The Liberator* he declared:

"I am aware that many object to the severity of my language; but is there not cause for severity? I will be as harsh as truth, and as uncompromising as justice. On this subject, I do not wish to think, or speak, or write, with moderation. No! No! Tell a man whose house is on fire to give a moderate alarm; tell him to moderately rescue his wife from the hands of the ravisher; tell the mother to gradually extricate her babe from the fire into which it has fallen;—but urge me not to use moderation in a cause like the present. I am in earnest—I will not equivocate—I will not excuse—I will not retreat a single inch—AND I WILL BE HEARD." [14]

White Virginians blamed Garrison for stirring up slaves and instigating slave rebellions like Nat Turner's.

The same year Garrison started publishing *The Liberator* he founded the New England Anti-Slavery Society. Two years later, he founded the American Anti-Slavery Society (AASS). The AASS rested their mission for immediate emancipation "upon the Declaration of our Independence, and upon the truths of Divine Revelation," binding their cause to both national and Christian redemption. Abolitionists fought to save slaves and their nation's soul. [2] By 1838, the AASS had 250,000 members, sometimes called Garrisonians. [11]

In order to spread their arguments against slavery based on moral suasion, abolitionists employed every method of outreach and agitation. At home in the North, abolitionists established hundreds of other antislavery societies and worked with long-

standing associations of black activists to establish schools, churches, and voluntary associations. Women and men of all colors were encouraged to associate together in these spaces to combat what they termed "color phobia."

Harnessing the potential of steam-powered printing and mass communication, abolitionists also blanketed the free states with pamphlets and antislavery newspapers. They blared their arguments from lyceum podiums and broadsides. Prominent individuals such as Wendell Phillips and Angelina Grimké saturated northern media with shame-inducing exposés of northern complicity in the return of fugitive slaves, and white reformers sentimentalized slave narratives that tugged at middle-class heartstrings. Abolitionists used the United States Postal Service in 1835 to inundate southern slaveholders' with calls to emancipate their slaves in order to save their souls, and, in 1836, they prepared thousands of petitions for Congress as part of the "Great Petition Campaign." In the six years from 1831 to 1837, abolitionist activities reached dizzying heights.

Such efforts encountered fierce opposition, however, as most Americans did not share abolitionists' particular brand of nationalism. In fact, abolitionists remained a small, marginalized group detested by most white Americans in both the North and the South. Immediatists were attacked as the harbingers of disunion, rabble-rousers who would stir up sectional tensions and thereby imperil the American experiment of self-government. Particularly troubling to some observers was the public engagement of women as abolitionist speakers and activists. Fearful of disunion and outraged by the interracial nature of abolitionism, northern mobs smashed abolitionist printing presses and inflicted violence on the movement's leaders. [2]

Garrison nearly lost his life in 1835 when a Boston anti-abolitionist mob dragged him through the city streets. A mob in Illinois killed an abolitionist named Elijah Lovejoy in 1837, and the following year, ten thousand protestors destroyed the abolitionists' newly built Pennsylvania Hall in Philadelphia, burning it to the ground. [11] White southerners, believing that abolitionists had incited Nat Turner's rebellion in 1831, aggressively purged antislavery dissent from the region.

Violent harassment threatened abolitionists' personal safety. In Congress, Whigs and Democrats joined forces in 1836 to pass an unprecedented restriction on freedom of political expression known as the "gag rule," prohibiting all discussion of abolitionist petitions in the House of Representatives. Two years later, mobs attacked the Anti-Slavery Convention of American Women, throwing rocks through the windows and burning the newly constructed Pennsylvania Hall to the ground.

In the face of such substantial external opposition, the abolitionist movement began to splinter. In 1839, an ideological schism shook the foundations of organized antislavery. Moral suasionists, led most prominently by William Lloyd Garrison, felt that the United States Constitution was a fundamentally pro-slavery document, and that the present political system was irredeemable. They dedicated their efforts exclusively towards persuading the public to redeem the nation by re-establishing it on antislavery grounds. However, many abolitionists, reeling from the level of entrenched opposition met in the 1830s, began to feel that moral suasion was no longer realistic. Instead, they believed, abolition would have to be effected through existing political processes. So, in 1839, political abolitionists formed the Liberty Party under the leadership of James G. Birney. This new abolitionist society was predicated on the belief that the U.S. Constitution was actually an antislavery document that could be used to abolish the stain of slavery through the national political system.

Another significant shift stemmed from the disappointments of the 1830s. Abolitionists in the 1840s increasingly moved from agendas based on reform to agendas based on resistance. Moral suasionists continued to appeal to hearts and minds, and political abolitionists launched sustained campaigns to bring abolitionist agendas to the ballot box. Meanwhile the entrenched and violent opposition of both slaveholders and the northern public encouraged abolitionists to find other avenues of fighting the slave power. Increasingly, for example, abolitionists focused on helping and protecting runaway slaves, and on establishing international antislavery support networks to help put pressure on the United States to abolish the institution. [2]

6.5: Frederick Douglass

Frederick Douglass

Frederick Douglass is one prominent example of how these trends: helping and protecting runaway slaves; and establishing international antislavery support networks to help put pressure on the United States to abolish the institution, came together. [2] Douglass was born a slave in Maryland in 1818 and escaped to New York in 1838. He later moved to New Bedford, Massachusetts, with his wife.

After escaping from slavery, Douglass soon came to the forefront of the abolitionist movement as a gifted orator and a powerful narrator of his experiences as a slave. Douglass's commanding presence and powerful speaking skills electrified his listeners when he began to provide public lectures on slavery. He came to the attention of William Lloyd Garrison and others who encouraged him to write his story. In 1845, he published his autobiography, *Narrative of the Life of Frederick Douglass, An American Slave Written by Himself* , in which he told about his life of slavery in Maryland. It was perhaps the most powerful and famous piece of African American literature from the nineteenth century. It was so widely read that it was reprinted in nine editions and translated into several languages. In it, Douglass identified by name the whites who had brutalized him, and for that reason, along with the mere act of publishing his story, Douglass had to flee the United States to avoid being murdered. [11] He traveled to Great Britain and met with famous British abolitionists like Thomas Clarkson, drumming up moral and financial support from British and Irish antislavery societies. He was neither the first nor the last runaway slave to make this voyage, but his great success abroad contributed significantly to rousing morale among weary abolitionists at home. [2]

British abolitionist friends ultimately bought his freedom from his Maryland owner, and Douglass returned to the United States. He began to publish his own abolitionist newspaper, *North Star* , in Rochester, New York. During the 1840s and 1850s, Douglass fought to bring about the end of slavery by telling the story of his life and highlighting how slavery destroyed families, both black and white. [11]

In this excerpt from *Narrative of the Life of Frederick Douglass* , he explains the consequences for the children fathered by white masters and slave women:

"Slaveholders have ordained, and by law established, that the children of slave women shall in all cases follow the condition of their mothers... this is done too obviously to administer to their own lusts, and make a gratification of their wicked desires profitable as well as pleasurable... the slaveholder, in cases not a few, sustains to his slaves the double relation of master and father... Such slaves [born of white masters] invariably suffer greater hardships... They are... a constant offence to their mistress... she is never better pleased than when she sees them under the lash, ... The master is frequently compelled to sell this class of his slaves, out of deference to the feelings of his white wife; and, cruel as the deed may strike any one to be, for a man to sell his own children to human flesh-mongers, ... for, unless he does this, he must not only whip them himself, but must stand by and see one white son tie up his brother, of but few shades darker ... and ply the gory lash to his naked back." [11]

Other abolitionists also spread word of the horrors of slavery in an attempt to win more supporters for their cause. A prominent example of this is Harriet Beecher Stowe, author of *Uncle Tom's Cabin* , or *Life Among the Lowly* . Stowe, a white woman from a pious Connecticut family, had strong moral convictions that slavery as an institution was evil and unnatural. Her book depicted the harsh conditions in which slaves lived, the danger they were willing to place themselves in to escape, and the detrimental ways in which the institution of slavery effected slave owners.*Uncle Tom's Cabin* was a success in the North, selling more than 300,000 copies in the first nine months of its publication, and more than a million copies by 1853. Nonetheless, it was met with protest and alarm in the South. [12]

The Underground Railroad

Many American abolitionists also took an active role in opposing slavery by supporting the Underground Railroad. Though illegal under the Fugitive Slave Law of 1850, participants such as former slaves Harriet Tubman, Henry Highland Garnet, Alexander Crummell, Amos Noë Freeman, and others put themselves at risk to help slaves escape to freedom. [12]

The Underground Railroad was a network of secret routes and safe houses used by nineteenth-century black slaves in the United States to escape to Northern free states and Canada with the aid of abolitionists and those sympathetic to their cause.

The term is also applied to the abolitionists—black and white, free and enslaved—who aided the fugitives. Some routes led to Mexico or overseas. The network was formed in the early nineteenth century and reached its height between 1850 and 1860. One estimate suggests that by 1850, 100,000 slaves had escaped via the "Railroad."

The origins of the Underground Railroad go back to the Compromise of 1850, passed by Congress after the Mexican-American War, which created a more stringent Fugitive Slave Act. The Fugitive Slave Act compelled officials of free states to assist slave catchers if there were runaway slaves in the area and granted slave catchers national immunity when in free states to do their job. Additionally, it made it possible that free blacks of the North could be forced into slavery even if they had been freed earlier or never been slaves at all because suspected slaves were unable to defend themselves in court and it was difficult to prove a free status. As a de facto bribe, judges were paid more ($10) for a decision that forced a suspected slave back into slavery than for a decision finding the slave to be free ($5). Thus, many Northerners who would have otherwise been able and content to ignore the persistence of slavery in the South chafed under what they saw as a national sanction on slavery, comprising one of the primary grievances of the Union cause during the Civil War.

*The various routes to freedom on the Underground Railroad.*Figure 6-5: Underground Railroad by Unknown is in the Public Domain .

The escape network of the Underground Railroad was not literally underground or a railroad. It was figuratively "underground" in the sense of being a covert form of resistance. It came to be referred to as a "railroad" due to the use of rail terminology in the code used by its participants. The Underground Railroad consisted of meeting points, secret routes, transportation, safe houses, and assistance provided by abolitionists and sympathizers. Individuals were often organized in small, independent groups. These small groups helped to maintain secrecy because individuals knew some connecting "stations" along the route but few details of their immediate area. Escaped slaves would move north along the route from one way station to the next. "Conductors" on the railroad came from various backgrounds and included free-born blacks, white abolitionists, former slaves (both runaways and manumitted), and Native Americans. Churches often played a role, especially the Society of Friends (Quakers), Congregationalists, Wesleyans, and Reformed Presbyterians, as well as certain sects of mainstream denominations such as the Methodist church and American Baptists.

To reduce the risk of infiltration, many people associated with the Underground Railroad knew only their part of the operation and little to nothing of the whole scheme. Written directions were discouraged for the same reason. Additionally, because many freedom seekers could not read, visual and audible clues such as patterns in quilts, song lyrics, and star positions provided directional cues along the way. Conductors moved the runaways from station to station. Often the conductor would pretend to be a slave to enter a plantation. Once a part of a plantation, the conductor would direct the runaways to the North.

Slaves would travel at night around 10 to 20 miles to each station or "depot," resting spots where the runaways could sleep and eat. The stations were out of the way places such as barns and were held by "station masters" who would provide assistance such as sending messages to other stations and directing fugitives on the path to take to their next stop. There were also those known as "stockholders" who gave money or supplies for assistance.

Figure 6-6: A Ride for Liberty – The Fugitive Slaves by Eastman Johnson has no known copyright restrictions.

Due to the risk of discovery, information about routes and safe havens was passed along by word of mouth. Southern newspapers of the day were often filled with pages of notices soliciting information about escaped slaves and offering sizable rewards for their capture and return. Federal marshals and professional bounty hunters known as "slave catchers" pursued fugitives as far as the Canadian border.

The risk was not limited solely to actual fugitives. Because strong, healthy black people in their prime working and reproductive years were treated as highly valuable commodities, it was not unusual for free blacks—both freedmen and those who had never been slaves—to be kidnapped and sold into slavery. "Certificates of freedom"—signed, notarized statements attesting to the free status of individuals—easily could be destroyed and thus afforded their holders little protection. Under the terms of the Fugitive Slave Act of 1850, when suspected fugitives were seized and brought to a special magistrate known as a "commissioner," they had no right to a jury trial and could not testify on their own behalf. The marshal or private slave catcher needed only to swear an oath to acquire a writ of replevin for the return of property.

Estimates vary widely, but at least 30,000 slaves, and potentially more than 100,000, escaped to Canada via the Underground Railroad. The largest group settled in Upper Canada, called Canada West from 1841 and known today as Southern Ontario, where numerous black Canadian communities developed. Upon arriving at their destinations, many fugitives were disappointed. Despite the British colonies' abolition of slavery in 1834, discrimination was still common.

With the outbreak of the Civil War in the United States, many black refugees enlisted in the Union Army, and while some later returned to Canada, many remained in the United States. Thousands of others returned to the American South after the war ended. The desire to reconnect with friends and family was strong and most were hopeful about the changes emancipation and Reconstruction would bring. [12]

Conclusion

As the 1850s progressed, abolitionist reform took a backseat as armed mobs protected runaway slaves in the North and fortified abolitionists engaged in bloody skirmishes in the West. Culminating in John Brown's raid on Harper's Ferry in 1859, the violence of the 1850s convinced many Americans that the issue of slavery was pushing the nation to the brink of sectional cataclysm. After two decades of immediatist agitation, the idealism of revivalist perfectionism had given way to a protracted battle for the moral soul of the country.

For all of the problems that abolitionism faced, the movement was far from a failure. The prominence of African Americans in abolitionist organizations offered a powerful, if imperfect, model of interracial coexistence. While immediatists always remained a minority, their efforts paved the way for the moderately antislavery Republican Party to gain traction in the years preceding the Civil War. It is hard to imagine that Abraham Lincoln could have become president in 1860 without the ground prepared by antislavery advocates and without the presence of radical abolitionists against whom he could be cast as a moderate alternative. Though it ultimately took a civil war to break the bonds of slavery in the United States, the evangelical moral compass of revivalist Protestantism provided motivation for the embattled abolitionists. [2]

CC licensed content, Shared previously

- The American YAWP. **Provided by**: Stanford University Press. **Located at**: http://www.americanyawp.com/index.html. **License**: *CC BY-SA: Attribution-ShareAlike*
- U.S. History. **Provided by**: OpenStax. **Located at**: https://cnx.org/contents/p7ovuIkl@6.2:gMXC1GEM@4/Introduction. **License**: *CC BY: Attribution*
- Boundless US History. **Provided by**: Lumen Learning. **Located at**: https://courses.lumenlearning.com/boundless-ushistory/. **License**: *CC BY-SA: Attribution-ShareAlike*

Public domain content

- Underground Railroad. **Located at**: commons.wikimedia.org/wiki/File:Undergroundrailroadsmall2.jpg. **License**: *Public Domain: No Known Copyright*
- A Ride for Liberty - The Fugitive Slaves. **Authored by**: Eastman Johnson. **Located at**: commons.wikimedia.org/wiki/File:Brooklyn_Museum_-_A_Ride_for_Liberty_--_The_Fugitive_Slaves_-_Eastman_Johnson_-_overall.jpg. **License**: *Public Domain: No Known Copyright*

6.6: Primary Sources

Primary Source Document: David Walker's Appeal to the Colored Citizens of the World 1829
Document Download Link

Primary Source Document: William Lloyd Garrison Introduces *The Liberator*
Document Download Link

CC licensed content, Original

- **Authored by**: Florida State College at Jacksonville. **License**: *CC BY: Attribution*

Public domain content

- David Walker, Walker's Appeal (Boston: David Walker, 1830). **Located at**: http://docsouth.unc.edu/nc/walker/walker.html/en-en/menu.html. **License**: *Public Domain: No Known Copyright*
- A memorial of William Lloyd Garrison from the city of Boston. **Provided by**: Boston (Mass.) City Council. **Located at**: https://archive.org/details/memorialofwillia01bost. **License**: *Public Domain: No Known Copyright*

CHAPTER OVERVIEW

7: THE WESTWARD EXPANSION OF SLAVERY

7.1: Introduction

The Westward Expansion of Slavery

Module Introduction

The creation of the cotton kingdom during the first half of the nineteenth century transformed the lives of African Americans, often for the worse. One of the most consequential inventions in American history, Eli Whitney's cotton gin from 1794, made large-scale cotton agriculture profitable. White planters and farmers from eastern seaboard states such as Virginia and North Carolina coveted lands in newer states to the southwest such as Alabama and Mississippi for their fertile soils and long growing seasons. Due in part to the growth of the cotton kingdom, nine new slave states entered the Union between 1789 and 1860, rapidly expanding and transforming the South into a region of economic growth built on slave labor. [4]

In addition to new land, white farmers and planters demanded large numbers of slaves for clearing land and planting and picking cotton. Since the international slave trade was outlawed in 1808, planters now purchased slaves internally from traders in a process known as the domestic slave trade. African-American slave labor in the South's cotton fields generated tremendous wealth for the region's small slave-holding elite. By the 1850s, slaves in the South produced 75% of the world's cotton. (Roche, 9) [1]

The creation of the cotton kingdom intensified the strain and trauma endured by slaves who feared being sold into the Deep South to work on often brutal cotton plantations and separated from family and friends. As always, African-Americans resisted slavery's dehumanizing forces by creating strong kinship or social networks and maintaining unique cultural traditions. [4]

Works Cited

Julian Roche, *The International Cotton Trade* (Cambridge, England: Woodhead Publishing, 1994), 9.

Learning Outcomes

This module addresses the following Course Learning Outcomes listed in the Syllabus for this course:

- To provide students with a general understanding of the history of African Americans within the context of American History.
- To motivate students to become interested and active in African American history by comparing current events with historical information.[1]

Additional learning outcomes associated with this module are:

- The student will be able to discuss the origins, evolution, and spread of racial slavery.
- The student will be able to describe the creation of a distinct African-American culture and how that culture became part of the broader American culture. [1]

Module Objectives

Upon completion of this module, the student will be able to:

- Discuss two ways that the cotton kingdom transformed the lives of African Americans.
- Examine the legacy of cotton slavery. [1]

Readings and Resources

Learning Unit: The Creation of the Cotton Kingdom (see below) [1]

CC licensed content, Original

- **Authored by**: Florida State College at Jacksonville. **License**: *CC BY: Attribution*

Public domain content

- The American Revolution. **Provided by**: National Park Service. **Located at**: www.nps.gov/revwar/index.html. **License**: *Public Domain: No Known Copyright*

7.2: The Creation Of The Cotton Kingdom

The Creation of the Cotton Kingdom

The Importance of Cotton

In November of 1785, the Liverpool firm of Peel, Yates, & Co. imported the first seven bales of American cotton ever to arrive in Europe. Prior to this unscheduled, and frankly unwanted, delivery, European merchants saw cotton as a product of the colonial Caribbean islands of Barbados, Saint-Domingue (now Haiti), Martinique, Cuba, and Jamaica. The American South, though relatively wide and expansive, was the go-to source for rice and, most importantly, tobacco.

Few knew that the seven bales sitting in Liverpool that winter of 1785 would change the world. But they did. By the early 1800s, the American South had developed a niche in the European market for "luxurious" long-staple cotton grown exclusively on the Sea Islands off the coast of South Carolina. But this was only the beginning of a massive flood to come, and the foundation of the South's astronomical rise to global prominence. Before long, botanists, merchants, and planters alike set out to develop strains of cotton seed that would grow further west on the Southern mainland, especially in the new lands opened up by the Louisiana Purchase of 1803—an area that stretched from New Orleans in the South to what is today Minnesota, parts of the Dakotas, and Montana. [2]

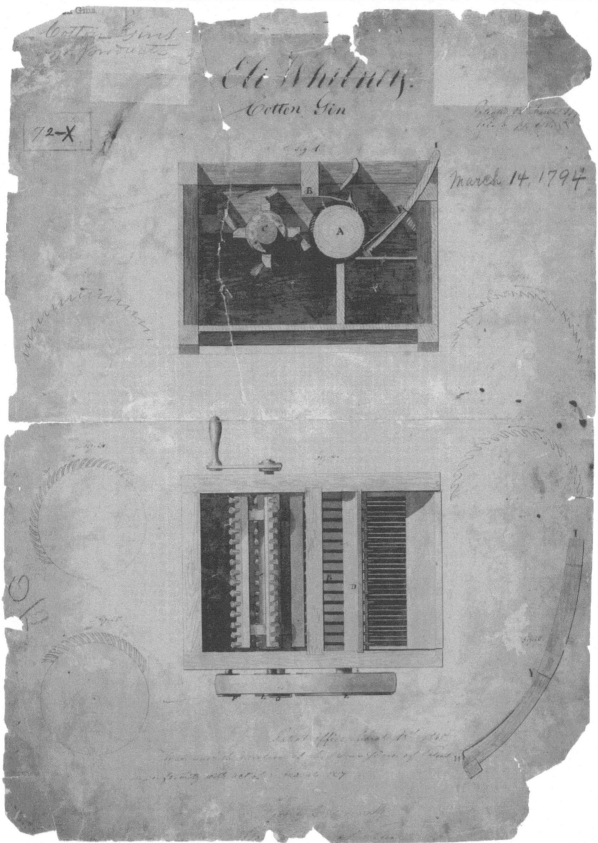

Figure 7-1: *Patent for Cotton Gin* by Eli Whitney is in the Public Domain .

*Model of Whitney's cotton gin displays cotton after the gin has removed the seeds from its boll.*Figure 7-2: Cotton gin EWM 2007 by Tom Murphy VII is in the Public Domain .

The discovery of Gossypium barbadense—often called "Petit Gulf" cotton—near Rodney, Mississippi, in 1820 changed the American and global cotton markets forever. "Petit Gulf," it was said, slid through the cotton gin—a machine developed by Eli Whitney in 1794 for deseeding cotton—more easily than any other strain. It also grew tightly, producing more usable cotton than anyone had imagined to that point. Perhaps most importantly, though, it came up at a time when Native peoples were being removed from the Southwest—southern Georgia, Alabama, Mississippi, and northern Louisiana. After Indian removal, land became readily available for white men with a few dollars and big dreams. Throughout the 1820s and 1830s, the federal government implemented several forced migrations of Native Americans, establishing a system of reservations west of the Mississippi River upon which all eastern peoples were required to relocate and settle. This, enacted through the Indian Removal Act of 1830, allowed the federal government to survey, divide, and auction off millions of acres of land for however much bidders were willing to pay. Suddenly, farmers with dreams of owning a large plantation could purchase dozens, even hundreds, of acres in the fertile Mississippi River Delta for cents on the dollar. Pieces of land that would cost thousands of dollars elsewhere sold in the 1830s for several hundred, at prices as low as 40¢ per acre.

Thousands of people, each with his or her own dream of massive and immediate success, rushed to the "Cotton Belt." Joseph Holt Ingraham, a writer and traveler from Maine, called it "mania." William Henry Sparks, a lawyer living in Natchez, Mississippi, remembered it as "a new El Dorado" in which "fortunes were made in a day, without enterprise or work." The change was astonishing. "Where yesterday the wilderness darkened over the land with her wild forests," he recalled, "to-day the cotton plantations whitened the earth." Money flowed from banks, many newly formed, on promises of "other-worldly" profits and overnight returns. Banks in New York City, Baltimore, Philadelphia, and even London offered lines of credit to anyone looking to buy land in the Southwest. Some even sent their own agents to purchase cheap land at auction for the express purpose of selling it, sometimes the very next day, at double and triple the original value, a process known as "speculation."

The explosion of available land in the fertile cotton belt brought new life to the South. By the end of the 1830s, "Petit Gulf" cotton had been perfected, distributed, and planted throughout the region.

Advances in steam power and water travel revolutionized Southern farmers' and planters' ability to deseed, bundle, and move their products to ports popping up along the Atlantic seaboard. Indeed, by the end of the 1830s, cotton had become the primary crop not only of the Southwestern states, but of the entire nation.

The numbers were staggering. In 1793, just a few years after the first, albeit unintentional, shipment of American cotton to Europe, the South produced around five million pounds of cotton, again almost exclusively the product of South Carolina's Sea Islands. Seven years later, in 1800, South Carolina remained the primary cotton producer in the South, sending 6.5 million pounds of the luxurious long-staple blend to markets in Charleston, Liverpool, London, and New York. But as the tighter, more abundant, and vibrant "Petit Gulf" strain moved west with the dreamers, schemers, and speculators, the American South quickly became the world's leading cotton producer. By 1835, the five main cotton-growing states—South Carolina, Georgia, Alabama, Mississippi, and Louisiana—produced more than 500 million pounds of "Petit Gulf" for a global market stretching from New Orleans to New York to London, Liverpool, Paris and beyond. That 500 million pounds of cotton made up nearly 55 percent of the entire United States export market, a trend that continued nearly every year until the outbreak of the Civil War. Indeed, the two billion pounds of cotton produced in 1860 alone amounted to more than 60 percent of the United States' total exports for that year.

"Petit Gulf" cotton grew relatively quickly on cheap, widely available land. With the invention of the cotton gin in 1794, and the emergence of steam power three decades later, cotton became the average man's commodity, the product with which the United States could expand westward, producing and reproducing Thomas Jefferson's vision of an idyllic republic of small farmers—a nation in control of its land, reaping the benefits of honest, free, and self-reliant work, a nation of families and farmers, expansion and settlement. But this all came at a violent cost. With the democratization of land ownership through Indian Removal, federal auctions, readily available credit, and the seemingly universal dream of cotton's immediate profit, one of the South's lasting "traditions" became normalized and engrained. And by the 1860s, that very "tradition," seen as the backbone of Southern society and culture, would split the nation in two. The heyday of American slavery had arrived. [2]

Cotton and Slavery

The rise of cotton, and the resulting upsurge in the United States' global position, wed the South to slavery. Without slavery there could be no "Cotton Kingdom," no massive production of raw materials stretching across thousands of acres worth millions of dollars. Indeed, cotton grew alongside slavery. The two moved hand-in-hand. The existence of slavery, and its importance to the Southern economy, became the defining factor in what would be known as the "Slave South." Although slavery arrived in the Americas long before cotton became a profitable commodity, the use and purchase of slaves, the moralistic and economic justifications for the continuation of slavery, even the urgency to protect the practice from extinction before the Civil War all received new life from the rise of cotton and the economic, social, and cultural growth spurt that accompanied its success.

Slavery had existed in the South since at least 1619, when a group of Dutch traders arrived at Jamestown with 20 Africans. Although these Africans remained under the ambiguous legal status of "unfree," rather than actual slaves, their arrival set in motion a practice that would stretch across the entire continent over the next two centuries. Slavery was everywhere by the time the American Revolution created the United States, although Northern states began a process of gradually abolishing the practice soon thereafter. In the more rural, agrarian South, slavery became a way of life, especially as farmers expanded their lands, planted more crops, and entered into the international trade market. By 1790, four years after the ratification of the Constitution, 654,121 slaves lived in the South—then just Virginia, North Carolina, South Carolina, Georgia, and the "Southwest Territory" (now Tennessee). Just twenty years later, in 1810, that number had increased to more than 1.1 million individuals in bondage.

The massive change in the South's enslaved population between 1790 and 1810 makes sense, though. During that time, the South went from a region of four states and one rather small territory to a region of six states (Virginia, North and South Carolina, Georgia, Kentucky, and Tennessee) and three rather large territories (Mississippi, Louisiana, and Orleans). The free population of the South also nearly doubled over that period—from around 1.3 million in 1790 to more than 2.3 million in 1810. It is important to note here that the enslaved population of the South did not increase at any rapid rate over the next two decades, until the cotton boom took hold in the mid-1830s. Indeed, following the constitutional ban on the international slave trade in 1808, the number of slaves in the South increased by just 750,000 in twenty years.

But then cotton came, and grew, and changed everything. Over the course of the 1830s, 40s, and 50s, slavery became so endemic to the "Cotton Belt" that travelers, writers, and statisticians began referring to the area as the "Black Belt," not only to

describe the color of the rich land, but also to describe the skin color of those forced to work its fields, line its docks, and move its products.

Perhaps the most important aspect of Southern slavery during this so-called "Cotton Revolution" was the value placed upon both the work and the body of the slaves themselves. Once the fever of the initial land rush subsided, land values became more static, and credit less free-flowing. For Mississippi land that in 1835 cost no more than $600, a farmer or investor would have to shell out more than $3,000 in 1850. By 1860, that same land, depending on its record of production and location, could cost as much as $100,000. In many cases, cotton growers, especially planters with large lots and enslaved workforces, put up slaves as collateral for funds dedicated to buying more land. If that land, for one reason or another, be it weevils, a late freeze, or a simple lack of nutrients, did not produce a viable crop within a year, the planter would lose not only the new land, but also the slaves he or she put up as a guarantee of payment.

So much went into the production of cotton, the expansion of land, and maintenance of enslaved workforces that by the 1850s, nearly every ounce of credit offered by Southern, and even Northern, banks dealt directly with some aspect of the cotton market. Millions of dollars changed hands. Slaves, the literal and figurative backbones of the Southern cotton economy, served as the highest and most important expense for any successful cotton grower. Prices for slaves varied drastically, depending on skin color, sex, age, and location, both of purchase and birth. In Virginia in the 1820s, for example, a single female slave of childbearing years sold for an average of $300; an unskilled man above the age of 18 sold for around $450; and boys and girls below 13 years sold for between $100 and $150.

By the 1840s, and into the 1850s, prices had nearly doubled—a result of both standard inflation and the increasing importance of enslaved laborers in the cotton market. In 1845, "plow boys" under the age of 18 sold for more than $600 in some areas, measured at "five or six dollars per pound." "Prime field hands," as they were called by merchants and traders, averaged $1,600 at market by 1850, a figure that fell in line with the rising prices of the cotton they picked. For example, when cotton sat at 7¢ per pound in 1838, the average "field hand" cost around $700. As the price of cotton increased to 9¢, 10¢, then 11¢ per pound over the next ten years, the average cost of an enslaved male laborer likewise rose to $775, $900, and then more than $1,600. [2]

*An African-American family picking cotton in a field near Savannah, Georgia in 1867 – two years after the abolition of slavery.*Figure 7-3: Picking Cotton, Savannah, Ga, early Negro life by Launey & Goebel has no known copyright restrictions.

   HUMANITIES

The key is that cotton and slaves helped define each other, at least in the cotton South. By the 1850s, slavery and cotton had become so intertwined, that the very idea of change—be it crop diversity, anti-slavery ideologies, economic diversification, or the increasingly staggering cost of purchasing and maintaining slaves—became anathema to the Southern economic and cultural identity. Cotton had become the foundation of the Southern economy. Indeed, it was the only major product, besides perhaps sugar cane in Louisiana, that the South could effectively market internationally.

As a result, Southern planters, politicians, merchants, and traders became more and more dedicated—some would say "obsessed"—to the means of its production: slaves and slavery. In 1834, Joseph Ingraham wrote that "to sell cotton in order to buy negroes—to make more cotton to buy more negroes, 'ad infinitum,' is the aim and direct tendency of all the operations of the thorough going cotton planter; his whole soul is wrapped up in the pursuit." Twenty-three years later, such pursuit had taken a seemingly religious character, as James Stirling, an Englishman traveling through the South, observed, "[slaves] and cotton—cotton and [slaves]; these are the law and the prophets to the men of the South."

The Cotton Revolution was a time of capitalism, panic, stress, and competition. Planters expanded their lands, purchased slaves, extended lines of credit, and went into massive amounts of debt because they were constantly working against the next guy, the newcomer, the social mover, the speculator, the trader. A single bad crop could cost even the wealthiest planter his or her entire life, along with those of his or her slaves and their families. Although the cotton market was large and profitable, it was also fickle, risky, and cost intensive. The more wealth one gained, the more land he or she needed to procure, which led to more slaves, more credit, and more mouths to feed. The decades before the Civil War in the South, then, were not times of slow, simple tradition. They were times of high competition, high risk, and high reward, no matter where one stood in the social hierarchy. But the risk was not always economic in nature.

The most tragic, indeed horrifying, aspect of slavery was its inhumanity. All slaves had memories, emotions, experiences, and thoughts. They saw their experiences in full color, felt the pain of the lash, the heat of the sun, and the heartbreak of loss, whether through death, betrayal, or sale. Communities developed upon a shared sense of suffering, common work, and even family ties. Slaves communicated in the slave markets of the urban South, and worked together to help their families, ease their loads, or simply frustrate their owners. Simple actions of resistance, such as breaking a hoe, running a wagon off the road, causing a delay in production due to injury, running away, or even pregnancy, provided a language shared by nearly all slaves in the agricultural workforce, a sense of unity that remained unsaid, but was acted out daily.

Beyond the basic and confounding horror of it all, the problem of slavery in the cotton South was twofold. First, and most immediate, was the fear and risk of rebellion. With nearly four million individual slaves residing in the South in 1860, and nearly 2.5 million living in the "Cotton Belt" alone, the system of communication, resistance, and potential violence among slaves did not escape the minds of slaveholders across the region and nation as a whole. As early as 1787, Thomas Jefferson wrote in his Notes on the State of Virginia that black and white people were "two warring nations" held at bay by the existence of slavery. If white slaveholders did not remain vigilant, Jefferson wrote, the presence of Africans in the Americas would "produce convulsions, which will probably never end but in the extermination of the one or the other race."

Southern writers, planters, farmers, merchants, and politicians expressed the same fears more than a half century later. "The South cannot recede," declared an anonymous writer in an 1852 issue of the New Orleans-based De Bow's Review. "She must fight for her slaves or against them. Even cowardice would not save her." To many slaveholders in the South, slavery was the saving grace not only of their own economic stability, but also the maintenance of peace and security in everyday life. Much of pro-slavery ideology rested upon the notion that slavery provided a sense of order, duty, and legitimacy to the lives of individual slaves, feelings that Africans and African Americans, it was said, could not otherwise experience. Without slavery, many thought, "blacks" (the word most often used for "slaves" in regular conversation) would become violent, aimless, and uncontrollable.

Some commentators recognized the problem in the 1850s, as the internal, or domestic, slave trade, the legal trade of slaves between states, along rivers, and along the Atlantic coastline. The internal trade picked up in the decade before the Civil War. The problem was rather simple. The more slaves one owned, the more money it cost to a) maintain them, and b) extract product from their work. As planters and cotton growers expanded their lands and purchased more slaves, their expectations increased.

And productivity, in large part, did increase. But it came on the backs of slaves with heavier workloads, longer hours, and more intense punishments. "The great limitation to production is labor," wrote one commentator in the American Cotton Planter in 1853. And many planters recognized this limitation, and worked night and day, sometimes literally, to find the

furthest extent of that limit. According to some contemporary accounts, by the mid 1850s, the expected production of an individual slave in Mississippi's Cotton Belt had increased from between four and five bales (weighing about 500 pounds each) per day to between eight and ten bales per day, on average. Other, perhaps more reliable sources, such as the account book of Buena Vista Plantation in Tensas Parish, Louisiana, list average daily production at between 300 and 500 pounds "per hand," with weekly averages ranging from 1,700 to 2,100 pounds "per hand." Cotton production "per hand" increased by 600 percent in Mississippi between 1820 and 1860. Each slave, then, was working longer, harder hours to keep up with his or her master's expected yield. [2]

*Stereograph image from Florida cotton circa 1870*Figure 7-4: A pyramid of cotton seed, Florida by B.W. Kilburn is in the Public Domain .

Here was capitalism with its most colonial, violent, and exploitative face. Humanity became a commodity used and worked to produce profit for a select group of investors, regardless of its shortfalls, dangers, and immoralities. But slavery, profit, and cotton did not exist only in the rural South. The Cotton Revolution sparked the growth of an urban South. The region's burgeoning cities served as Southern hubs of a global market, conduits through which the work of slaves and the profits of planters met and funded a wider world. [2]

CC licensed content, Shared previously

- The American YAWP. **Provided by**: Stanford University Press. **Located at**: http://www.americanyawp.com/index.html. **License**: *CC BY-SA: Attribution-ShareAlike*

Public domain content

- Patent for Cotton Gin. **Authored by**: Eli Whitney. **Located at**: commons.wikimedia.org/wiki/File:Patent_for_Cotton_Gin_(1794)_-_hi_res.jpg. **License**: *Public Domain: No Known Copyright*
- Cotton gin EWM 2007. **Authored by**: Tom Murphy VII. **Located at**: commons.wikimedia.org/wiki/File:Cotton_gin_EWM_2007.jpg. **License**: *Public Domain: No Known Copyright*
- Picking Cotton, Savannah, Ga, early Negro life . **Authored by**: Launey & Goebel . **Located at**: commons.wikimedia.org/wiki/File:Picking_cotton,_Savannah,_Ga.,_early_Negro_life_LCCN2015650292.tif. **License**: *Public Domain: No Known Copyright*
- A pyramid of cotton seed, Floridau00a0. **Authored by**: B.W. Kilburn. **Located at**: commons.wikimedia.org/wiki/File:A_pyramid_of_cotton_seed,_Florida,_by_Kilburn,_B._W._(Benjamin_West),_1827-

7.3: The Domestic Slave Trade

The Domestic Slave Trade

The South's dependence on cotton was matched by its dependence on slaves to harvest the cotton. Despite the rhetoric of the Revolution that "all men are created equal," slavery not only endured in the American republic but formed the very foundation of the country's economic success. Cotton and slavery occupied a central—and intertwined—place in the nineteenth-century economy.

In 1807, the U.S. Congress abolished the foreign slave trade, a ban that went into effect on January 1, 1808. After this date, importing slaves from Africa became illegal in the United States. While smuggling continued to occur, the end of the international slave trade meant that domestic slaves were in very high demand. Fortunately for Americans whose wealth depended upon the exploitation of slave labor, a fall in the price of tobacco had caused landowners in the Upper South to reduce their production of this crop and use more of their land to grow wheat, which was far more profitable. While tobacco was a labor-intensive crop that required many people to cultivate it, wheat was not. Former tobacco farmers in the older states of Virginia and Maryland found themselves with "surplus" slaves whom they were obligated to feed, clothe, and shelter. Some slaveholders responded to this situation by freeing slaves; far more decided to sell their excess bondsmen. Virginia and Maryland therefore took the lead in the domestic slave trade, the trading of slaves within the borders of the United States. (11)

*A group of slaves, also known as a coffle, being marched from Virginia to Tennessee by white slave traders in the domestic slave trade.*Figure 7-5: *Slave Trader, Sold to Tennessee* by Unknown is in the Public Domain .

The text on the image below reads:

(top of drawing)

Arise! Arise! and weep no more dry up your tears, we shall part no more. Come rose we go to Tennessee, that happy shore, to old Virginia never—never—return.

(bottom of drawing)

The Company going to Tennessee from Staunton, Augusta county, – the law of Virginia suffered them to go on. I was astonished at this boldness, the carrier stopped a moment. Then ordered the march, I saw the play it is commonly in this state, with the negro's in droves Sold.

The domestic slave trade offered many economic opportunities for white men. Those who sold their slaves could realize great profits, as could the slave brokers who served as middlemen between sellers and buyers. Other white men could benefit from the trade as owners of warehouses and pens in which slaves were held, or as suppliers of clothing and food for slaves on the move. Between 1790 and 1859, slaveholders in Virginia sold more than half a million slaves. In the early part of this period, many of these slaves were sold to people living in Kentucky, Tennessee, and North and South Carolina. By the 1820s, however, people in Kentucky and the Carolinas had begun to sell many of their slaves as well. Maryland slave dealers sold at least 185,000 slaves. Kentucky slaveholders sold some seventy-one thousand individuals. Most of the slave traders carried these slaves further south to Alabama, Louisiana, and Mississippi. New Orleans, the hub of commerce, boasted the largest slave market in the United States and grew to become the nation's fourth-largest city as a result. Natchez, Mississippi, had the second-largest market. In Virginia, Maryland, the Carolinas, and elsewhere in the South, slave auctions happened every day. (11)

*An 1840 advertisement by a slave trader for the sale of slaves at an auction in New Orleans, Louisiana.*Figure 7-6: *ValuableGangOfYoungNegroes1840* by Jos. A. Beard is in the Public Domain .

An 1853 painting by the English artist Eyre Crowe showing African American slaves in a slave market in Richmond, Virginia being auctioned to slave traders.Figure 7-7: Slaves Waiting for Sale – Richmond , Virginia by Eyre Crowe is in the Public Domain .

All told, the movement of slaves in the South made up one of the largest forced internal migrations in the United States. In each of the decades between 1820 and 1860, about 200,000 people were sold and relocated. The 1800 census recorded over one million African Americans, of which nearly 900,000 were slaves. By 1860, the total number of African Americans increased to 4.4 million, and of that number, 3.95 million were held in bondage. For many slaves, the domestic slave trade incited the terror of being sold away from family and friends. [11]

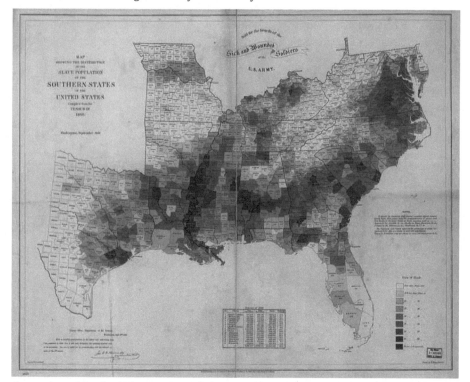

A map issued by the US Coast Guard showing the percentage of slaves in the population in each county in the slave-holding states of the United States in 1860. The note reads: It should be observed, that several counties appear comparatively light. This arises from the Preponderance of white and free blacks in the large towns in those counties, such as Henrico Co. Va... Charleston Co. S/C, etc. The figures in each county represent the percentage of slaves viz: Amherst Co, Va 46-7/10 are slaves in every 100 inhabitants; Wayne Co, N. Carolina 38-5/10 are slaves in every 100 inhabitants.Figure 7-9: SlavePopulationUS1860 by E. Hergesheimer and Th. Leonhardt is in the Public Domain *.*

Solomon Northup Remembers the New Orleans Slave Market

Solomon Northup was a free black man living in Saratoga, New York, when he was kidnapped and sold into slavery in 1841. He later escaped and wrote a book about his experiences: *Twelve Years a Slave. Narrative of Solomon Northup, a Citizen of*

New-York, Kidnapped in Washington City in 1841 and Rescued in 1853 (the basis of a 2013 Academy Award–winning film). This excerpt derives from Northup's description of being sold in New Orleans, along with fellow slave Eliza and her children Randall and Emily.

One old gentleman, who said he wanted a coachman, appeared to take a fancy to me… The same man also purchased Randall. The little fellow was made to jump, and run across the floor, and perform many other feats, exhibiting his activity and condition. All the time the trade was going on, Eliza was crying aloud, and wringing her hands. She besought the man not to buy him, unless he also bought her self and Emily… Freeman turned round to her, savagely, with his whip in his uplifted hand, ordering her to stop her noise, or he would flog her. He would not have such work—such snivelling; and unless she ceased that minute, he would take her to the yard and give her a hundred lashes… Eliza shrunk before him, and tried to wipe away her tears, but it was all in vain. She wanted to be with her children, she said, the little time she had to live. All the frowns and threats of Freeman, could not wholly silence the afflicted mother. [11]

CC licensed content, Shared previously

- U.S. History. **Provided by**: OpenStax. **Located at**: https://cnx.org/contents/p7ovuIkl@6.2:gMXC1GEM@4/Introduction. **License**: *CC BY: Attribution*

Public domain content

7.4: Life as a Slave in the Cotton Kingdom

Life as a Slave in the Cotton Kingdom

In addition to cotton, the great commodity of the antebellum South was human chattel. Slavery was the cornerstone of the southern economy. By 1850, about 3.2 million slaves labored in the United States, 1.8 million of whom worked in the cotton fields. Slaves faced arbitrary power abuses from whites; they coped by creating family and community networks. Storytelling, song, and Christianity also provided solace and allowed slaves to develop their own interpretations of their condition.

Southern whites frequently relied upon the idea of paternalism—the premise that white slaveholders acted in the best interests of slaves, taking responsibility for their care, feeding, discipline, and even their Christian morality—to justify the existence of slavery. This grossly misrepresented the reality of slavery, which was, by any measure, a dehumanizing, traumatizing, and horrifying human disaster and crime against humanity. Nevertheless, slaves were hardly passive victims of their conditions; they sought and found myriad ways to resist their shackles and develop their own communities and cultures. [11]

Figure 7-10: Cotton planter and pickers 1908 by H. Tees is in the Public Domain .

Slaves often used the notion of paternalism to their advantage, finding opportunities within this system to engage in acts of resistance and win a degree of freedom and autonomy. For example, some slaves played into their masters' racism by hiding their intelligence and feigning childishness and ignorance. The slaves could then slow down the workday and sabotage the system in small ways by "accidentally" breaking tools, for example; the master, seeing his slaves as unsophisticated and childlike, would believe these incidents were accidents rather than rebellions. Some slaves engaged in more dramatic forms of resistance, such as poisoning their masters slowly. Other slaves reported rebellious slaves to their masters, hoping to gain preferential treatment. Slaves who informed their masters about planned slave rebellions could often expect the slaveholder's gratitude and, perhaps, more lenient treatment. Such expectations were always tempered by the individual personality and caprice of the master.

Slaveholders used both psychological coercion and physical violence to prevent slaves from disobeying their wishes. Often, the most efficient way to discipline slaves was to threaten to sell them. The lash, while the most common form of punishment, was effective but not efficient; whippings sometimes left slaves incapacitated or even dead. Slave masters also used punishment gear like neck braces, balls and chains, leg irons, and paddles with holes to produce blood blisters. Slaves lived in constant terror of both physical violence and separation from family and friends.

Under southern law, slaves could not marry. Nonetheless, some slaveholders allowed marriages to promote the birth of children and to foster harmony on plantations. Some masters even forced certain slaves to form unions, anticipating the birth of more children (and consequently greater profits) from them. Masters sometimes allowed slaves to choose their own

partners, but they could also veto a match. Slave couples always faced the prospect of being sold away from each other, and, once they had children, the horrifying reality that their children could be sold and sent away at any time.

Slave parents had to show their children the best way to survive under slavery. This meant teaching them to be discreet, submissive, and guarded around whites. Parents also taught their children through the stories they told. Popular stories among slaves included tales of tricksters, sly slaves, or animals like Brer Rabbit, who outwitted their antagonists. Such stories provided comfort in humor and conveyed the slaves' sense of the wrongs of slavery. Slaves' work songs commented on the harshness of their life and often had double meanings—a literal meaning that whites would not find offensive and a deeper meaning for slaves. [11]

Work Song Example 1: Slow Drag Work Song by John A. Lomax (Collector) has no known copyright restrictions. [17]

Work Song Example 2: Long Hot Summer Day by John A. Lomax (Collector) has no known copyright restrictions. [18]

*Gordon, pictured here with scars and welts on his back from whippings he received as a slave, endured terrible brutality from his master before escaping to Union Army lines in 1863. He would become a soldier and help fight to end the violent system that produced the horrendous scars on his back.*Figure 7-11: *Gordon, scourged back* by Mathew Brady is in the Public Domain .

African beliefs, including ideas about the spiritual world and the importance of African healers, survived in the South as well. Whites who became aware of non-Christian rituals among slaves labeled such practices as witchcraft. Among Africans, however, the rituals and use of various plants by respected slave healers created connections between the African past and the American South while also providing a sense of community and identity for slaves. Other African customs, including traditional naming patterns, the making of baskets, and the cultivation of certain native African plants that had been brought to the New World, also endured. [4]

The concept of family, more than anything else, played a crucial role in the daily lives of slaves. Family and kinship networks, and the benefits they carried, represented an institution through which slaves could piece together a sense of community, a sense of feeling and dedication, separate from the forced system of production that defined their daily lives. The creation of family units, distant relations, and communal traditions allowed slaves to maintain religious beliefs, ancient ancestral traditions, and even names passed down from generation to generation in a way that challenged enslavement. Ideas passed between relatives on different plantations, names given to children in honor of the deceased, and basic forms of love and devotion created a sense of individuality, an identity that assuaged the loneliness and desperation of enslaved life. Family defined how each plantation, each community, functioned, grew, and labored.

Marriage served as the single most important aspect of cultural and identity formation, as it connected slaves to their own pasts, and gave some sense of protection for the future. By the start of the Civil War, approximately two-thirds of slaves were members of nuclear households, each household averaging six people—mother, father, children, and often a grandparent, elderly aunt or uncle, and even "in-laws." Those who did not have a marriage bond, or even a nuclear family, still maintained family ties, most often living with a single parent, brother, sister, or grandparent.

Many slave marriages endured for many years. But the threat of disruption, often through sale, always loomed. As the domestic slave trade increased following the constitutional ban on slave importation in 1808 and the rise of cotton in the 1830s and 1840s, slave families, especially those established prior to the slaves' arrival in the United States, came under increased threat. Hundreds of thousands of marriages, many with children, fell victim to sale "downriver"—a euphemism for the near constant flow of slave laborers down the Mississippi River to the developing cotton belt in the Southwest. In fact, during the Cotton Revolution alone, between one-fifth and one-third of all slave marriages were broken up through sale or forced migration. But this was not the only threat. Planters, and slaveholders of all shapes and sizes, recognized that marriage was, in the most basic and tragic sense, a privilege granted and defined by them for their slaves. And as a result, many slaveholders used slaves' marriages, or the threats thereto, to squeeze out more production, counteract disobedience, or simply make a gesture of power and superiority.

Threats to family networks, marriages, and household stability did not stop with the death of a master. A slave couple could live their entire lives together, even having been born, raised, and married on the slave plantation, and, following the death of their master, find themselves at opposite sides of the known world. It only took a single relative, executor, creditor, or friend of the deceased to make a claim against the estate to cause the sale and dispersal of an entire slave community.

Enslaved women were particularly vulnerable to the shifts of fate attached to slavery. In many cases, female slaves did the same work as men, spending the day—from sun up to sun down—in the fields picking and bundling cotton. In some rare cases, especially among the larger plantations, planters tended to use women as house servants more than men, but this was not universal. In both cases, however, female slaves' experiences were different than their male counterparts, husbands, and neighbors. Sexual violence, unwanted pregnancies, and constant childrearing while continuing to work the fields all made life as a female slave more prone to disruption and uncertainty.

Harriet Jacobs, an enslaved woman from North Carolina, chronicled her master's attempts to sexually abuse her in her narrative, Incidents in the Life of a Slave Girl. Jacobs suggested that her successful attempts to resist sexual assault and her determination to love whom she pleased was "something akin to freedom." But this "freedom," however empowering and contextual, did not cast a wide net. Many enslaved women had no choice concerning love, sex, and motherhood. On plantations, small farms, and even in cities, rape was ever-present. Like the splitting of families, slaveholders used sexual violence as a form of terrorism, a way to promote increased production, obedience, and power relations. And this was not restricted only to unmarried women. In numerous contemporary accounts, particularly violent slaveholders forced men to witness the rape of their wives, daughters, and relatives, often as punishment, but occasionally as a sadistic expression of power and dominance.

As property, enslaved women had no recourse, and society, by and large, did not see a crime in this type of violence. Racist pseudo-scientists claimed that whites could not physically rape Africans or African Americans, as the sexual organs of each were not compatible in that way. State law, in some cases, supported this view, claiming that rape could only occur between either two white people or a black man and a white woman. All other cases fell under a silent acceptance. The consequences of rape, too, fell to the victim in the case of slaves. Pregnancies that resulted from rape did not always lead to a lighter workload for the mother. And if a slave acted out against a rapist, whether that be her master, mistress, or any other white attacker, her actions were seen as crimes rather than desperate acts of survival. For example, a 19-year-old slave named Celia fell victim to

repeated rape by her master in Callaway County, Missouri. Between 1850 and 1855, Robert Newsom raped Celia hundreds of times, producing two children and several miscarriages. Sick and desperate in the fall of 1855, Celia took a club and struck her master in the head, killing him. But instead of sympathy and aid, or even an honest attempt to understand and empathize, the community called for the execution of Celia. On November 16, 1855, after a trial of ten days, Celia, the 19-year-old rape victim and slave, was hanged for her crimes against her master.

Life on the ground in cotton South, like the cities, systems, and networks within which it rested, defied the standard narrative of the Old South. Slavery existed to dominate, yet slaves formed bonds, maintained traditions, and crafted new culture. They fell in love, had children, and protected one another using the privileges granted them by their captors, and the basic intellect allowed all human beings. They were resourceful, brilliant, and vibrant, and they created freedom where freedom seemingly could not exist. And within those communities, resilience and dedication often led to cultural sustenance. Among the enslaved, women, and the impoverished-but-free, culture thrived in ways that are difficult to see through the bales of cotton and the stacks of money sitting on the docks and in the counting houses of the South's urban centers. But religion, honor, and pride transcended material goods, especially among those who could not express themselves that way. [2]

7.5: The Free Black Population

The Free Black Population

Complicating the picture of the slavery in the antebellum South was the existence of a large free black population. In fact, more free blacks lived in the South than in the North; roughly 261,000 lived in slave states, while 226,000 lived in northern states without slavery. Most free blacks did not live in the Lower, or Deep South: the states of Alabama, Arkansas, Florida, Georgia, Louisiana, Mississippi, South Carolina, and Texas. Instead, the largest number lived in the upper southern states of Delaware, Maryland, Virginia, North Carolina, and later Kentucky, Missouri, Tennessee, and the District of Columbia.

*A late 18 th century collage painting of a free black woman with her quadroon daughter. They are wearing elaborate dresses that signify their relatively high social status as free people.*Figure 7-12: *Free Woman of Color with daughter* by Unknown is in the Public Domain .

Part of the reason for the large number of free blacks living in slave states were the many instances of manumission—the formal granting of freedom to slaves—that occurred as a result of the Revolution, when many slaveholders put into action the ideal that "all men are created equal" and freed their slaves. The transition in the Upper South to the staple crop of wheat, which did not require large numbers of slaves to produce, also spurred manumissions. Another large group of free blacks in the South had been free residents of Louisiana before the 1803 Louisiana Purchase, while still other free blacks came from Cuba and Haiti.

Most free blacks in the South lived in cities, and a majority of free blacks were lighter-skinned women, a reflection of the interracial unions that formed between white men and black women. Everywhere in the United States blackness had come to be associated with slavery, the station at the bottom of the social ladder. Both whites and those with African ancestry tended to delineate varying degrees of lightness in skin color in a social hierarchy. In the slaveholding South, different names described one's distance from blackness or whiteness: mulattos (those with one black and one white parent), quadroons (those with one black grandparent), and octoroons (those with one black great-grandparent). Lighter-skinned blacks often looked down on their darker counterparts, an indication of the ways in which both whites and blacks internalized the racism of the age.

Some free blacks in the South owned slaves of their own. Andrew Durnford, for example, was born in New Orleans in 1800, three years before the Louisiana Purchase. His father was white, and his mother was a free black. Durnford became an American citizen after the Louisiana Purchase, rising to prominence as a Louisiana sugar planter and slaveholder. William

Ellison, another free black who amassed great wealth and power in the South, was born a slave in 1790 in South Carolina. After buying his freedom and that of his wife and daughter, he proceeded to purchase his own slaves, whom he then put to work manufacturing cotton gins. By the eve of the Civil War, Ellison had become one of the richest and largest slaveholders in the entire state.

The phenomenon of free blacks amassing large fortunes within a slave society predicated on racial difference, however, was exceedingly rare. Most free blacks in the South lived under the specter of slavery and faced many obstacles. Beginning in the early nineteenth century, southern states increasingly made manumission of slaves illegal. They also devised laws that divested free blacks of their rights, such as the right to testify against whites in court or the right to seek employment where they pleased. Interestingly, it was in the upper southern states that such laws were the harshest. In Virginia, for example, legislators made efforts to require free blacks to leave the state. In parts of the Deep South, free blacks were able to maintain their rights more easily. The difference in treatment between free blacks in the Deep South and those in the Upper South, historians have surmised, came down to economics. In the Deep South, slavery as an institution was strong and profitable. In the Upper South, the opposite was true. The anxiety of this economic uncertainty manifested in the form of harsh laws that targeted free blacks. (11)

Conclusion

Cotton transformed the South into the most profitable and powerful slave society in world history. The commodity opened a previously closed society to the grandeur, the profit, the exploitation, and the social dimensions of a larger, more connected, global community. By 1860, not only did the South produce three quarters of the world's cotton it held in bondage nearly 4 million slaves worth more than 3 billion dollars, or 13 trillion in 2016 dollars. Nothing was more valuable in the United States other than the land itself. The cotton kingdom generated not only tremendous wealth, it also deepened the sectional fault lines between North and South during the first half of the nineteenth-century. Northern states looked on with dread as slavery continued spread and threatened to dominate land out west that Thomas Jefferson and other founders envisioned as an "empire of liberty," a land reserved free white farmers. As slavery spread into new territories and then states, Northern politicians feared that slaveholders and their interests would dominate Congress and corrupt American democracy. Southerners argued vehemently that the Constitution protected their property rights, which included slaves, and allowed them to spread slavery anywhere they wished. The cotton kingdom, and with it the westward expansion of slavery, thus set the stage for the sectional crisis of the nineteenth century. (Huston, 27) [1]

CHAPTER OVERVIEW

8: SLAVERY AND THE SECTIONAL CRISIS

8.1: Introduction

Slavery and the Sectional Crisis

Module Introduction

Slavery's western expansion created problems for the United States from the very start. Battles emerged over the westward expansion of slavery and over the role of the federal government in protecting the interests of slaveholders. Northern workers felt that slavery suppressed wages and stole land that could have been used by poor white Americans to achieve economic independence. Southerners feared that without slavery's expansion, the abolitionist faction would come to dominate national politics and an increasingly dense population of slaves would lead to bloody insurrection and race war.

Constant resistance from enslaved men and women required a strong proslavery government to maintain order. As the North gradually abolished human bondage, enslaved men and women headed North on an underground railroad of hideaways and safe houses. Northerners and Southerners came to disagree sharply on the role of the federal government in capturing and returning these freedom seekers. While Northerners appealed to their states' rights to refuse capturing runaway slaves, Southerners demanded a national commitment to slavery. Enslaved laborers meanwhile remained vitally important to the nation's economy, fueling not only the southern plantation economy but also providing raw materials for the industrial North.

Differences over the fate of slavery remained at the heart of American politics, especially as the United States expanded. After decades of conflict, Americans north and south began to fear that the opposite section of the country had seized control of the government. By November 1860, an opponent of slavery's expansion arose from within the Republican Party. During the secession crisis that followed, fears, nearly a century in the making, at last devolved into bloody war. [2]

Learning Outcomes

This module addresses the following Course Learning Outcomes listed in the Syllabus for this course:

- To provide students with a general understanding of the history of African Americans within the context of American History.
- To motivate students to become interested and active in African American history by comparing current events with historical information.[1]

Additional learning outcomes associated with this module are:

- The student will be able to discuss the origins, evolution, and spread of racial slavery.
- The student will be able to describe the creation of a distinct African-American culture and how that culture became part of the broader American culture. [1]

Module Objectives

Upon completion of this module, the student will be able to:

- Identify issues related to slavery that divided the north and south in the 19th century.
- Discuss the sectional crisis between the north and the south. [1]

Readings and Resources

Learning Unit: The Sectional Crisis (see below) [1]

CC licensed content, Original
- **Authored by**: Florida State College at Jacksonville. **License**: *CC BY: Attribution*

CC licensed content, Shared previously
- The American YAWP. **Provided by**: Stanford University Press. **Located at**: http://www.americanyawp.com/index.html. **License**: *CC BY-SA: Attribution-ShareAlike*

8.2: The Sectional Crisis

The Sectional Crisis

Sectionalism in the Early Republic

Slavery's history stretched back to antiquity. Prior to the American Revolution, nearly everyone in the world accepted it as a natural part of life. English colonies north and south relied on enslaved workers who grew tobacco, harvested indigo and sugar, and worked in ports. They generated tremendous wealth for the British crown. That wealth and luxury fostered seemingly limitless opportunities, and inspired seemingly boundless imaginations. Enslaved workers also helped give rise to revolutionary new ideals, ideals that in time became the ideological foundations of the sectional crisis. English political theorists, in particular, began to re-think natural law justifications for slavery. They rejected the longstanding idea that slavery was a condition that naturally suited some people. A new transatlantic antislavery movement began to argue that freedom was the natural condition of man.

Revolutionaries seized onto these ideas to stunning effect in the late eighteenth century. In the United States, France, and Haiti, revolutionaries began the work of splintering the old order. Each revolution seemed to radicalize the next. Bolder and more expansive declarations of equality and freedom followed one after the other. Revolutionaries in the United States declared, "All men are created equal," in the 1770s. French visionaries issued the "Declaration of Rights and Man and Citizen" by 1789. But the most startling development came in 1803. A revolution led by the island's rebellious slaves turned France's most valuable sugar colony into an independent country administered by the formerly enslaved.[2]

Attack and take of the Crête-à-Pierrot—1803 Battle of Vertiéres. Haitian rebel forces, comprised of liberated slaves, fight Napoleon's expeditionary forces. Figure 8-1: *Haitian Revolution* by Auguste Raffet is in the Public Domain .

The Haitian Revolution marked an early origin of the sectional crisis. It helped splinter the Atlantic basin into clear zones of freedom and un-freedom, shattering the longstanding assumption that African-descended slaves could not also be rulers.

Despite the clear limitations of the American Revolution in attacking slavery, the era marked a powerful break in slavery's history. Military service on behalf of both the English and the American army freed thousands of slaves. Many others simply used the turmoil of war to make their escape. As a result, free black communities emerged—communities that would continually reignite the antislavery struggle. For nearly a century, most white Americans were content to compromise over the issue of slavery, but the constant agitation of black Americans, both enslaved and free, kept the issue alive.

The national breakdown over slavery occurred over a long timeline and across a broad geography. Debates over slavery in the American West proved especially important. As the United States pressed westward, new questions arose as to whether those lands ought to be slave or free. The framers of the Constitution did a little, but not much, to help resolve these early questions. Article VI of the 1787 Northwest Ordinance banned slavery north and west of the Ohio River. Many took it to mean that the founders intended for slavery to die out, as why else would they prohibit its spread across such a huge swath of territory?

Debates over the framer's intentions often led to confusion and bitter debate, but the actions of the new government left better clues as to what the new nation intended for slavery. Congress authorized the admission of Vermont (1791) and Kentucky (1792), with Vermont coming into the Union as a free state, and Kentucky coming in as a slave state. Though Americans at the time made relatively little of the balancing act suggested by the admission of a slave state and a free state, the pattern became increasingly important. By 1820, preserving the balance of free states and slave states would be seen as an issue of national security.

New pressures challenging the delicate balance again arose in the West. The Louisiana Purchase of 1803 more than doubled the size of the United States. Questions immediately arose as to whether these lands would be made slave or free. Complicating matters further was the rapid expansion of plantation slavery fueled by the invention of the cotton gin in 1793. Yet even with the booming cotton economy, many Americans, including Thomas Jefferson, believed that slavery was a temporary institution and would soon die out. Tensions rose with the Louisiana Purchase, but a truly sectional national debate remained mostly dormant.

That debate, however, came quickly. Sectional differences tied to the expansion of plantation slavery in the West were especially important after 1803. The Ohio River Valley became an early fault line in the coming sectional struggle. Kentucky and Tennessee emerged as slave states, while free states Ohio, Indiana (1816) and Illinois (1818) gained admission along the river's northern banks. Borderland negotiations and accommodations along the Ohio River fostered a distinctive kind of white supremacy, as laws tried to keep blacks out of the West entirely. Ohio's so-called "Black Laws," of 1803 foreshadowed the exclusionary cultures of Indiana, Illinois, and several subsequent states of the Old Northwest and later, the Far West. These laws often banned African American voting, denied black Americans access to public schools, and made it impossible for non-whites to serve on juries and in local militias, among a host of other restrictions and obstacles.

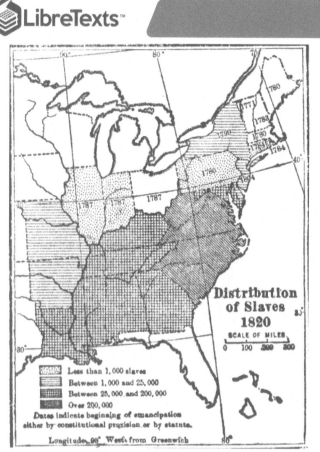

*Map showing the distribution of slaves in the United States in 1820.*Figure 8-2: *Slavery US 1820* by Allen Johnson is in the Public Domain .

The Missouri Territory, by far the largest section of the Louisiana Territory, marked a turning point in the sectional crisis. Saint Louis, a bustling Mississippi River town filled with powerful slave owners, loomed large as an important trade headquarters for networks in the northern Mississippi Valley and the Greater West. In 1817, eager to put questions of whether this territory would be slave or free to rest, Congress opened its debate over Missouri's admission to the Union. Congressman James Tallmadge of New York proposed laws that would gradually abolish slavery in the new state. Southern states responded with unanimous outrage, and the nation shuddered at an undeniable sectional controversy.

Congress reached a "compromise" on Missouri's admission, largely through the work of Kentuckian Henry Clay. Maine would be admitted to the Union as a free state. In exchange, Missouri would come into the Union as a slave state. Legislators sought to prevent future conflicts by making Missouri's southern border at 36° 30′ the new dividing line between slavery and freedom in the Louisiana Purchase lands. South of that line, running east from Missouri to the western edge of the Louisiana Purchase lands (near the present-day Texas panhandle) slavery could expand. North of it, encompassing what in 1820 was still "unorganized territory," there would be no slavery.

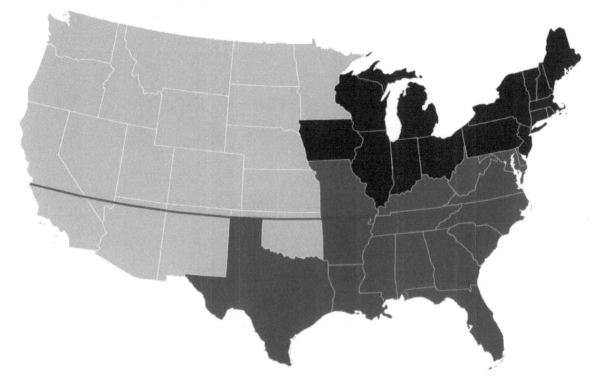

*(1820) Slave states, including Missouri, in red and the free states in blue. The green line is the Missouri Compromise line.*Figure 8-3: *Missouri Compromise Line* by Júlio Reis is licensed under CC BY-SA 3.0 .

The Missouri Compromise marked a major turning point in America's sectional crisis because it exposed to the public just how divisive the slavery issue had grown. The debate filled newspapers, speeches, and Congressional records. Antislavery and pro-slavery positions from that point forward repeatedly returned to points made during the Missouri debates. Legislators battled for weeks over whether the Constitutional framers intended slavery's expansion or not, and these contests left deep scars. Even seemingly simple and straightforward phrases like "All Men Are Created Equal" were hotly contested all over again. Questions over the expansion of slavery remained open, but nearly all Americans concluded that the Constitution protected slavery where it already existed.

Southerners were not yet advancing arguments that said slavery was a positive good, but they did insist during the Missouri Debate that the framers supported slavery and wanted to see it expand. In Article 1, Section 2, for example, the Constitution enabled representation in the South to be based on rules defining enslaved people as $^3/_5$ of a voter, meaning southern white men would be overrepresented in Congress. The Constitution also stipulated that Congress could not interfere with the slave trade before 1808, and enabled Congress to draft fugitive slave laws.

Antislavery participants in the Missouri debate argued that the framers never intended slavery to survive the Revolution and in fact hoped it would disappear through peaceful means. The framers of the Constitution never used the word "slave." Slaves were referred to as "persons held in service," perhaps referring to English common law precedents that questioned the legitimacy of "property in man." Antislavery activists also pointed out that while the Congress could not pass a law limiting the slave trade by 1808, the framers had also recognized the flip side of the debate and had thus opened the door to legislating the slave trade's end once the deadline arrived. Language in the Tenth Amendment, they claimed, also said slavery could be banned in the territories. Finally, they pointed to the due process clause of the Fifth Amendment, which said that property could be seized through appropriate legislation. The bruising Missouri debates ultimately transcended arguments about the Constitution. They became an all-encompassing referendum on the American past, present, and future.

Despite the furor, the Missouri Crisis did not yet inspire hardened defenses of either slave or free labor as positive good. Those would come in the coming decades. In the meantime, the uneasy consensus forged by the Missouri Debate managed to bring a measure of calm.

The Missouri debate had also deeply troubled the nation's African Americans and Native Americans. By the time of the Missouri compromise debate, both groups saw that whites never intended them to be citizens of the United States. In fact, the

debates over Missouri's admission had offered the first sustained debate on the question of black citizenship, as Missouri's State Constitution wanted to impose a hard ban on any future black migrants. Legislators ultimately agreed that this hard ban violated the Constitution, but reaffirmed Missouri's ability to deny citizenship to African Americans. Americans by 1820 had endured a broad challenge, not only to their cherished ideals but also more fundamentally to their conceptions of self. [2]

8.3: The Crisis Joined

The Crisis Joined

Missouri's admission to the Union in 1821 exposed deep fault lines in American society. But the Compromise created a new sectional consensus that most white Americans, at least, hoped would ensure a lasting peace. Through sustained debates and arguments, white Americans agreed that the Constitution could do little about slavery where it already existed and that slavery, with the State of Missouri as the key exception, would never expand north of the 36°30′ line.

Once again westward expansion challenged this consensus, and this time the results proved even more damaging. Tellingly, enslaved southerners were among the first to signal their discontent. A rebellion led by Denmark Vesey in 1822 threatened lives and property throughout the Carolinas. The nation's religious leaders also expressed a rising discontent with the new status quo. [9] The Second Great Awakening further sharpened political differences by promoting schisms within the major Protestant churches, schisms that also became increasingly sectional in nature. Between 1820 and 1846, sectionalism drew on new political parties, new religious organizations, and new reform movements.

As politics grew more democratic, leaders attacked old inequalities of wealth and power, but in doing so many pandered to a unity under white supremacy. Slavery briefly receded from the nation's attention in the early 1820s, but that would change quickly. By the last half of the decade, slavery was back, and this time it appeared even more threatening.

Inspired by the social change of Jacksonian democracy, white men regardless of status would gain not only land and jobs, but also the right to vote, the right to serve on juries, the right to attend public schools, and the right to serve in the militia and armed forces. In this post-Missouri context, leaders arose to push the country's new expansionist desires in aggressive new directions. As they did so, however, the sectional crisis again deepened.

The Democratic Party initially seemed to offer a compelling answer to the problems of sectionalism by promising benefits to white working men of the North, South, and West, while also uniting rural, small town, and urban residents. Indeed, huge numbers of western, southern, and northern workingmen rallied during the 1828 Presidential election behind Andrew Jackson. The Democratic Party tried to avoid the issue of slavery and instead sought to unite Americans around shared commitments to white supremacy and desires to expand the nation.

Democrats were not without their critics. Northerners seen as especially friendly to the South had become known as "Doughfaces" during the Missouri debates, and as the 1830s wore on, more and more Doughfaced Democrats became vulnerable to the charge that they served the Southern slave oligarchs better than they served their own northern communities. Whites discontented with the direction of the country used the slur and other critiques to help chip away at Democratic Party majorities. The accusation that northern Democrats were lap dogs for southern slaveholders had real power.

The Whigs offered an organized major party challenge to the Democrats. Whig strongholds often mirrored the patterns of westward migrations out of New England. Whigs drew from an odd coalition of wealthy merchants, middle and upper class farmers, planters in the Upland South, and settlers in the Great Lakes. Because of this motley coalition, the party struggled to bring a cohesive message to voters in the 1830s. Their strongest support came from places like Ohio's Western Reserve, the rural and Protestant-dominated areas of Michigan, and similar parts of Protestant and small-town Illinois, particularly the fast-growing towns and cities of the state's northern half.

Whig leaders stressed Protestant culture, federal-sponsored internal improvements, and courted the support of a variety of reform movements, including temperance, nativism, and even antislavery, though few Whigs believed in racial equality. These positions attracted a wide range of figures, including a young convert to politics named Abraham Lincoln. Lincoln admired Whig leader Henry Clay of Kentucky, and by the early 1830s, Lincoln certainly fit the image of developing Whig. A veteran of the Black Hawk War, Lincoln had re-located to New Salem, Illinois, where he worked a variety of odd jobs, living a life of thrift, self-discipline, and sobriety as he educated himself in preparation for a professional life in law and politics.

The Whig Party blamed Democrats for defending slavery at the expense of the American people, but antislavery was never a core component of the Whig platform. Several abolitionists grew so disgusted with the Whigs that they formed their own party, a true antislavery party. Activists in Warsaw, New York organized the antislavery Liberty Party in 1839. Liberty leaders demanded the end of slavery in the District of Columbia, the end of the interstate slave trade, and the prohibition of slavery's expansion into the West. But the Liberty Party also shunned women's participation in the movement and distanced themselves

from visions of true racial egalitarianism. Few Americans voted for the party. The Democrats and Whigs continued to dominate American politics.

Democrats and Whigs fostered a moment of relative calm on the slavery debate, partially aided by gag rules prohibiting discussion of antislavery petitions. Arkansas (1836) and Michigan (1837) became the newest states admitted to the Union, with Arkansas coming in as a slave state, and Michigan coming in as a free state. Michigan gained admission through provisions established in the Northwest Ordinance, while Arkansas came in under the Missouri Compromise. Since its lands were below the line at 36° 30′ the admission of Arkansas did not threaten the Missouri consensus. The balancing act between slavery and freedom continued.

Events in Texas would shatter the balance. Independent Texas soon gained recognition from a supportive Andrew Jackson administration in 1837. But Jackson's successor, President Martin Van Buren, also a Democrat, soon had reasons to worry about the Republic of Texas. Texas struggled with ongoing conflicts with Mexico and Indian raids from the powerful Comanche. The 1844 democratic presidential candidate James K. Polk sought to bridge the sectional divide by promising new lands to whites north and south. Polk cited the annexation of Texas and the Oregon Territory as campaign cornerstones. Yet as Polk championed the acquisition of these vast new lands, northern Democrats grew annoyed by their southern colleagues, especially when it came to Texas.

For many observers, the debates over Texas statehood illustrated that the federal government was clearly pro-slavery. Texas President Sam Houston managed to secure a deal with Polk, and gained admission to the Union for Texas in 1845. Antislavery northerners also worried about the admission of Florida, which entered the Union as a slave state in 1845. The year 1845 became a pivotal year in the memory of antislavery leaders. As Americans embraced calls to pursue their "Manifest Destiny," antislavery voices looked at developments in Florida and Texas as signs that the sectional crisis had taken an ominous and perhaps irredeemable turn.

The 1840s opened with a number of disturbing developments for antislavery leaders. The 1842 Supreme Court case *Prigg v. Pennsylvania* ruled that the federal government's Fugitive Slave Act trumped Pennsylvania's personal liberty law. Antislavery activists believed that the federal government only served southern slaveholders and were trouncing the states' rights of the North. A number of northern states reacted by passing new personal liberty laws in protest in 1843.

The year 1846 signaled new reversals to the antislavery cause, and the beginnings of a dark new era in American politics. President Polk and his Democratic allies were eager to see western lands brought into the Union and were especially anxious to see the borders of the nation extended to the shores of the Pacific Ocean. Critics of the administration blasted these efforts as little more than land-grabs on behalf of slaveholders. Events in early 1846 seemed to justify antislavery complaints. Since Mexico had never recognized independent Texas, it continued to lay claim to its lands, even after the United States admitted it to the Union. In January 1846, Polk ordered troops to Texas to enforce claims stemming from its border dispute along the Rio Grande. Polk asked for war on May 11, 1846, and by September 1847, the United States had invaded Mexico City. Whigs, like Abraham Lincoln, found their protests sidelined, but antislavery voices were becoming more vocal and more powerful.

After 1846, the sectional crisis raged throughout North America. Debates swirled over whether the new lands would be slave or free. The South began defending slavery as a positive good. At the same time, Congressman David Wilmot submitted his "Wilmot Proviso" late in 1846, banning the expansion of slavery into the territories won from Mexico. The Proviso gained widespread northern support and even passed the House with bipartisan support, but it failed in the Senate. [2]

CC licensed content, Shared previously

8.4: Free Soil, Free Labor, Free Men

Free Soil, Free Labor, Free Men

The conclusion of the Mexican War gave rise to the 1848 Treaty of Guadeloupe Hidalgo. The treaty infuriated antislavery leaders in the United States. The spoils gained from the Mexican War were impressive, and it was clear they would help expand slavery. The United States required Mexican officials to cede the California and New Mexico Territories for $15 million dollars. With American soldiers occupying their capital, Mexican leaders had no choice but sign or continue fighting a war they could not win. The new American territory included lands that would become the future states of California, Utah, Nevada, most of Arizona, and well as parts of New Mexico, Colorado, and Wyoming.

Map showing the states and territories of the United States in 1848, including the Mexican Cession—land acquired from Mexico following the Mexican War and the Treaty of Guadalupe Hidalgo (1848).Figure 8-4: United States 1848 by Golbez is licensed under CC BY-SA 3.0 .

The acquisition of so much land made it imperative to antislavery leaders that these lands not be opened to slavery. But knowing that the Liberty Party was not likely to provide a home to many moderate voters, leaders instead hoped to foster a new and more competitive party, which they called the Free Soil Party. Antislavery leaders entered the 1848 election hoping that their vision of a federal government divorced from slavery might be heard. But both the Whigs and the Democrats, nominated pro-slavery southerners. Left unrepresented, antislavery Free Soil leaders swung into action.

Demanding an alternative to the pro-slavery status quo, Free Soil leaders assembled so-called "Conscience Whigs." The new coalition called for a national convention in August 1848 at Buffalo, New York. A number of ex-Democrats committed to the party right away, including an important group of New Yorkers loyal to Martin Van Buren. The Free Soil Party's platform bridged the eastern and the western leadership together and called for an end to slavery in Washington DC and a halt on slavery's expansion in the territories. The Free Soil movement hardly made a dent in the 1848 Presidential election, but it drew more than four times the popular vote won by the Liberty Party earlier. It was a promising start. In 1848, Free Soil leaders claimed just 10% of the popular vote, but won over a dozen House seats, and even managed to win one Senate seat in Ohio,

which went to Salmon P. Chase. In Congress, Free Soil members had enough votes to swing power to either the Whigs or the Democrats.

The admission of Wisconsin as a free state in May 1848 helped cool tensions after the Texas and Florida admissions. But news from a number of failed revolutions in Europe alarmed American reformers. As exiled radicals filtered out of Europe and into the United States, a women's rights movement also got underway at Seneca Falls, New York. Representing the first of such meetings ever held in United States history, it was led by figures like Elizabeth Cady Stanton and Lucretia Mott, women with deep ties to the abolitionist cause. Frederick Douglass also appeared at the convention and took part in the proceedings, where participants debated the Declaration of Sentiments, Grievances and Resolutions.

By August 1848, it seemed plausible that the Free Soil Movement might tap into these reforms and build a broader coalition. In some ways that is precisely what it did. But come November, the spirit of reform failed to yield much at the polls. Whig candidate Zachary Taylor bested Democrat Lewis Cass of Michigan.

The upheavals signaled by 1848 came to a quick end. Taylor remained in office only a brief time until his unexpected death from a stomach ailment in 1850. During Taylor's brief time in office, the fruits of the Mexican War began to spoil. While he was alive, Taylor and his administration struggled to find a good remedy. Increased clamoring for the admission of California, New Mexico, and Utah pushed the country closer to the edge. Gold had been discovered in California, and as thousands continued to pour onto the West Coast and through the trans-Mississippi West, the admission of new states loomed. In Utah, Mormons were also making claims to an independent state they called Deseret. By 1850, California wanted admission as a free state. With so many competing dynamics underway, and with the President dead and replaced by Whig Millard Fillmore, the 1850s were off to a troubling start.

Congressional leaders like Henry Clay and newer legislators like Stephen A. Douglas of Illinois were asked to broker a compromise, but this time it was clear no compromise could bridge all the diverging interests at play in the country. Clay eventually left Washington disheartened by affairs. It fell to young Stephen Douglas, then, to shepherd the bills through the Congress, which he in fact did. Legislators rallied behind the "Compromise of 1850," an assemblage of bills passed late in 1850, which managed to keep the promises of the Missouri Compromise alive.

Henry Clay ('The Great Compromiser') addresses the U.S. Senate during the debates over the Compromise of 1850. The print shows a number of incendiary personalities, like John C. Calhoun, whose increasingly sectional beliefs were pacified for a time by the Compromise. [2]Figure 8-5: *Henry Clay Senate* by Peter F. Rothermel is in the Public Domain .

The Compromise of 1850 tried to offer something to everyone, but in the end, it only worsened the sectional crisis. For southerners, the package offered a tough new fugitive slave law that empowered the federal government to deputize regular citizens in arresting runaways. The New Mexico territory and the Utah Territory, would be allowed to determine their own fates as slave or free states based on popular sovereignty. The Compromise also allowed territories to submit suits directly to the Supreme Court over the status of fugitive slaves within its bounds.

The admission of California as the newest free state in the Union cheered many northerners, but even the admission of a vast new state full of resources and rich agricultural lands was not enough. In addition to California, northerners also gained a ban on the slave trade in Washington, D.C., but not the full emancipation abolitionists had long advocated. Texas, which had already come into the Union as a slave state, was asked to give some of its land to New Mexico in return for the federal government absorbing some of the former republic's debt. But the Compromise debates soon grew ugly.

After the Compromise of 1850, antislavery critics became increasingly certain that slaveholders had co-opted the federal government, and that a southern "Slave Power" secretly held sway in Washington, where it hoped to make slavery a national institution. These northern complaints pointed back to how the $^3/_5$ compromise of the Constitution gave southerners more representatives in Congress. In the 1850s, antislavery leaders increasingly argued that Washington worked on behalf of slaveholders while ignoring the interests of white working men.

None of the individual 1850 Compromise measures proved more troubling to national and international observers than the Fugitive Slave Act. In a clear bid to extend slavery's influence throughout the country, the act created special federal commissioners to determine the fate of alleged fugitives without benefit of a jury trial or even court testimony. Under its

provisions, local authorities in the North could not interfere with the capture of fugitives. Northern citizens, moreover, had to assist in the arrest of fugitive slaves when called upon by federal agents. The Fugitive Slave Act created the foundation for a massive expansion of federal power, including an alarming increase in the nation's policing powers. Many northerners were also troubled by the way the bill undermined local and state laws. The law itself fostered corruption and the enslavement of free black northerners. The federal commissioners who heard these cases were paid $10 if they determined that the defendant was a slave and only $5 if they determined he or she was free. Many black northerners responded to the new law by heading further north to Canada.

The 1852 Presidential election gave the Whigs their most stunning defeat and effectively ended their existence as a national political party. Whigs captured just 42 of the 254 electoral votes needed to win. With the Compromise of 1850 and plenty of new lands, peaceful consensus seemed on the horizon. Antislavery feelings continued to run deep, however, and their depth revealed that with a Democratic Party misstep, a coalition united against the Democrats might yet emerge and bring them to defeat. One measure of the popularity of antislavery ideas came in 1852 when Harriet Beecher Stowe published her bestselling antislavery novel, *Uncle Tom's Cabin* . ((Harriet Beecher Stowe, *Uncle Tom's Cabin* (Boston: 1852).)) Sales for *Uncle Tom's Cabin* were astronomical, eclipsed only by sales of the Bible. The book became a sensation and helped move antislavery into everyday conversation for many northerners. Despite the powerful antislavery message, Stowe's book also reinforced many racist stereotypes. Even abolitionists struggled with the deeply ingrained racism that plagued American society. While the major success of Uncle Tom's Cabin bolstered the abolitionist cause, the terms outlined by the Compromise of 1850 appeared strong enough to keep the peace.

Democrats by 1853 were badly splintered along sectional lines over slavery, but they also had reasons to act with confidence. Voters had returned them to office in 1852 following the bitter fights over the Compromise of 1850. Emboldened, Illinois Senator Stephen A. Douglas introduced a set of additional amendments to a bill drafted in late 1853 to help organize the Nebraska Territory, the last of the Louisiana Purchase lands. In 1853, the Nebraska Territory was huge, extending from the northern end of Texas to the Canadian Border. Altogether, it encompassed present-day Nebraska, Wyoming, South Dakota, North Dakota, Colorado and Montana. Douglas's efforts to amend and introduce the bill in 1854 opened dynamics that would break the Democratic Party in two and, in the process, rip the country apart.

*Fullpage illustration from Uncle Tom's Cabin . Characters Eliza, Harry, Chloe, Tom, and Old Bruno. Eliza is coming to tell Uncle Tom he is to be sold and that she is running away with her child.*Figure 8-6: *ElizaEngraving* by Hammatt Billings is in the Public Domain .

Democrats by 1853 were badly splintered along sectional lines over slavery, but they also had reasons to act with confidence. Voters had returned them to office in 1852 following the bitter fights over the Compromise of 1850. Emboldened, Illinois Senator Stephen A. Douglas introduced a set of additional amendments to a bill drafted in late 1853 to help organize the Nebraska Territory, the last of the Louisiana Purchase lands. In 1853, the Nebraska Territory was huge, extending from the northern end of Texas to the Canadian Border. Altogether, it encompassed present-day Nebraska, Wyoming, South Dakota, North Dakota, Colorado and Montana. Douglas's efforts to amend and introduce the bill in 1854 opened dynamics that would break the Democratic Party in two and, in the process, rip the country apart.

Douglas proposed a bold plan in 1854 to cut off a large southern chunk of Nebraska and create it separately as the Kansas Territory. Douglas had a number of goals in mind. The expansionist Democrat from Illinois wanted to organize the territory to facilitate the completion of a national railroad that would flow through Chicago. But before he had even finished introducing

the bill, opposition had already mobilized. Salmon P. Chase drafted a response in northern newspapers that exposed the Kansas-Nebraska Bill as a measure to overturn the Missouri Compromise and open western lands for slavery. Kansas-Nebraska protests emerged in 1854 throughout the North, with key meetings in Wisconsin and Michigan. Kansas would become slave or free depending on the result of local elections, elections that would be greatly influenced by migrants flooding to the state to either protect or stop the spread of slavery.

Ordinary Americans in the North increasingly resisted what they believed to be a pro-slavery federal government on their own terms. The rescues and arrests of fugitive slaves Anthony Burns in Boston and Joshua Glover in Milwaukee, for example, both signaled the rising vehemence of resistance to the nation's 1850 fugitive slave law. The case of Anthony Burns illustrates how the Fugitive Slave Law radicalized many northerners. On May 24, 1854, 20-year-old Burns, a preacher who worked in a Boston clothing shop, was clubbed and dragged to jail. One year earlier, Burns had escaped slavery in Virginia, and a group of slave catchers had come to return him to Richmond. Word of Burns' capture spread rapidly through Boston, and a mob gathered outside of the courthouse demanding Burns' release. Two days after the arrest, the crowd stormed the courthouse and shot a Deputy U.S. Marshall to death. News reached Washington, and the federal government sent soldiers. Boston was placed under Martial Law. Federal troops lined the streets of Boston as Burns was marched to a ship where he was sent back to slavery in Virginia. After spending over $40,000, the United States Government had successfully reenslaved Anthony Burns. A short time later, Burns was redeemed by abolitionists who paid $1,300 to return him to freedom, but the outrage among Bostonians only grew. And Anthony Burns was only one of hundreds of highly publicized episodes of the federal governments imposing the Fugitive Slave Law on rebellious northern populations. In the words of Amos Adams Lawrence, "We went to bed one night old-fashioned, conservative, compromise Union Whigs & woke up stark mad Abolitionists."

As northerners radicalized, organizations like the New England Emigrant Aid Society provided guns and other goods for pioneers willing to go to Kansas and establish the territory as antislavery through popular sovereignty. On all sides of the slavery issue, politics became increasingly militarized.

The year 1855 nearly derailed the northern antislavery coalition. A resurgent anti-immigrant movement briefly took advantage of the Whig collapse, and nearly stole the energy of the anti-administration forces by channeling its frustrations into fights against the large number of mostly Catholic German and Irish immigrants in American cities. Calling themselves "Know-Nothings," on account of their tendency to pretend ignorance when asked about their activities, the Know-Nothing or American Party made impressive gains in 1854 and 1855, particularly in New England and the Middle Atlantic. But the anti-immigrant movement simply could not capture the nation's attention in ways the antislavery movement already had.

The antislavery political movements that started in 1854 coalesced as the coming Presidential election of 1856 accelerated the formation of a new political party. Harkening back to the founding fathers, this new party called itself the Republican Party. Republicans moved into a highly charged summer expecting great things for their cause. Following his explosive speech before Congress on May 19-20 in which he castigated Southern Democrats their complicity in the "crimes" occurring in Kansas, Charles Sumner was beaten by congressional representative Preston Brooks of South Carolina right on the floor of the Senate chamber. Among other accusations, Sumner accused Senator Andrew Butler of South Carolina of defending slavery so he could have sexual access to black women. Butler's cousin, representative Brooks felt that he had to defend his relative's honor, and nearly killed Sumner as a result.

An 1856 Lithograph showing Democratic Representative Preston Brooks beating Republican Senator Charles Sumner with a cane.Figure 8-8: *Southern Chivalry* by John L. Magee is in the Public Domain .

The violence in Washington pales before the many murders occurring in Kansas. Proslavery raiders attacked Lawrence, Kansas. Radical abolitionist John Brown retaliated, murdering several pro-slavery Kansans in retribution. As all of this played out, the House failed to expel Brooks. Brooks resigned his seat anyway, only to be re-elected by his constituents later in the year. He received new canes emblazoned with the words "Hit him again!"

With sectional tensions at a breaking point, both parties readied for the coming Presidential election. In June 1856, the newly named Republican Party held its nominating convention at Philadelphia, and selected Californian John Charles Frémont. Frémont's antislavery credentials may not have pleased many abolitionists, but his dynamic and talented wife, Jessie Benton Frémont, appealed to more radical members of the coalition. The Kansas-Nebraska Debate, the organization of the Republican Party, and the 1856 Presidential Campaign all energized a new generation of political leaders, including Abraham Lincoln. Beginning with his speech at Peoria, Illinois, in 1854, Lincoln carved out a message that encapsulated better than anyone else the main ideas and visions of the Republican Party. Lincoln himself was slow to join the coalition, yet by the summer of 1856, Lincoln had fully committed to the Frémont campaign.

Frémont lost, but Republicans celebrated that he won 11 of the 16 free states. This showing, they urged, was truly impressive for any party making its first run at the Presidency. Yet northern Democrats in crucial swing states remained unmoved by the Republican Party's appeals. Ulysses S. Grant of Missouri, for example, worried that Frémont and Republicans signaled trouble for the Union itself. Grant voted for the Democratic candidate, James Buchanan, believing a Republican victory might bring about disunion. In abolitionist and especially black American circles, Frémont's defeat was more than a disappointment. Believing their fate had been sealed as permanent non-citizens, some African Americans would consider foreign emigration and colonization. Others began to explore the option of more radical and direct action against the Slave Power. [2]

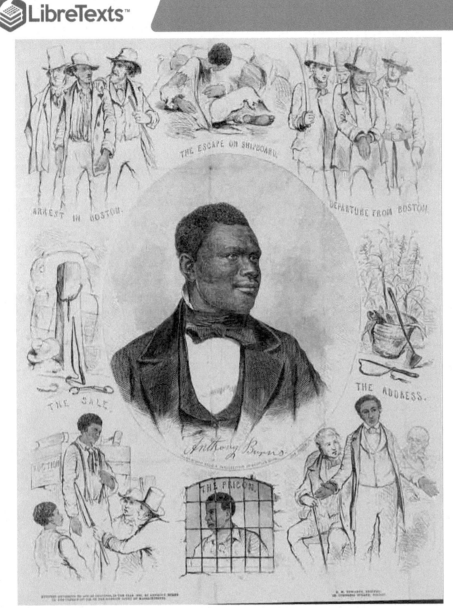

A bust portrait of the twenty-four-year-old Burns is surrounded by scenes from his life. These include (clockwise from lower left): the sale of the youthful Burns at auction, a whipping post with bales of cotton, his arrest in Boston on May 24, 1854, his escape from Richmond on shipboard, his departure from Boston escorted by federal marshals and troops, Burns's "address" (to the court?), and finally Burns in prison. Copyrighting works such as prints and pamphlets under the name of the subject (here Anthony Burns) was a common abolitionist practice. This was no doubt the case in this instance, since by 1855 Burns had in fact been returned to his owner in Virginia. Figure 8-7: *Anthony Burns* by R.M. Edwards is in the Public Domain.

CC licensed content, Shared previously

- The American YAWP. **Provided by**: Stanford University Press. **Located at**: http://www.americanyawp.com/index.html. **License**: *CC BY-SA: Attribution-ShareAlike*
- UNITED STATES 1848. **Authored by**: Golbez. **Located at**: commons.wikimedia.org/wiki/File:United_States_1848-05-1848-08.png. **License**: *CC BY-SA: Attribution-ShareAlike*

Public domain content

- HENRY CLAY SENATE. **Authored by**: Peter F. Rothermel . **Located at**: commons.wikimedia.org/wiki/File:Henry_Clay_Senate3.jpg. **License**: *Public Domain: No Known Copyright*
- ELIZAENGRAVING. **Authored by**: Hammatt Billings. **Located at**: commons.wikimedia.org/wiki/File:ElizaEngraving.jpg. **License**: *Public Domain: No Known Copyright*
- SOUTHERN CHIVALRY. **Authored by**: John L. Magee. **Located at**: commons.wikimedia.org/wiki/File:Southern_Chivalry.jpg. **License**: *Public Domain: No Known Copyright*

- ANTHONY BURNS. **Authored** by: R.M. Edwards. **Located** at: commons.wikimedia.org/wiki/File:Anthony_Burns_1.jpg. **License**: *Public Domain: No Known Copyright*

8.5: From Sectional Crisis to National Crisis

From Sectional Crisis to National Crisis

White antislavery leaders hailed Frémont's defeat as a "glorious" one and looked ahead to the party's future successes. For those still in slavery, or hoping to see loved ones freed, the news was of course much harder to take. The Republican Party had promised the rise of an antislavery coalition, but voters rebuked it. The lessons seemed clear enough.

Kansas loomed large over the 1856 election, darkening the national mood. The story of voter fraud in Kansas had begun years before in 1854, when nearby Missourians first started crossing the border to tamper with the Kansas elections. Noting this, critics at the time attacked the Pierce administration for not living up to the ideals of popular sovereignty by ensuring fair elections. From there, the crisis only deepened. Kansas voted to come into the Union as a free state, but the federal government refused to recognize their votes and instead recognized a sham pro-slavery legislature.

The sectional crisis had at last become a national crisis. "Bleeding Kansas" was the first place to demonstrate that the sectional crisis could easily, and in fact already was, exploding into a full-blown national crisis. As the national mood grew increasingly grim, Kansas attracted militants representing the extreme sides of the slavery debate.

In the days after the 1856 Presidential election, Buchanan made his plans for his time in office clear. He talked with Chief Justice Roger Taney on inauguration day about a court decision he hoped to see handled during his time in office. Indeed, not long after the inauguration, the Supreme Court handed down a decision that would come to define Buchanan's Presidency. The Dred Scott decision, *Scott v. Sandford* , ruled that black Americans could not be citizens of the United States. This gave the Buchanan administration and its southern allies a direct repudiation of the Missouri Compromise. The court ruled that Scott, a Missouri slave, had no right to sue in United States courts. The Dred Scott decision signaled that the federal government was now fully committed to extending slavery as far and as wide as it might want.

The Dred Scott decision seemed to settle the sectional crisis by making slavery fully national, but in reality it just exacerbated sectional tensions further. In 1857, Buchanan sent U.S. military forces to Utah, hoping to subdue Utah's Mormon communities. This action, however, led to renewed charges, many of them leveled from within his own party, that the administration was abusing its powers. Far more important than the Utah invasion, however, was the ongoing events in Kansas. It was Kansas that at last proved to many northerners that the sectional crisis would not go away unless slavery also went away.

The Illinois Senate race in 1858 put the scope of the sectional crisis on full display. Republican candidate Abraham Lincoln challenged the greatly influential Democrat Stephen Douglas. Pandering to appeals to white supremacy, Douglas hammered the Republican opposition as a "Black Republican" party bent on racial equality. The Republicans, including Lincoln, were thrown on the defensive. Democrats hung on as best they could, but the Republicans won the House of Representatives and picked up seats in the Senate. Lincoln actually lost his contest with Stephen Douglas, but in the process firmly established himself as a leading national Republican. After the 1858 elections, all eyes turned to 1860. Given the Republican Party's successes since 1854, it was expected that the 1860 Presidential election might produce the nation's first antislavery president.

In the troubled decades since the Missouri Compromise, the nation slowly tore itself apart. Congressman clubbed each other nearly to death on the floor of the Congress, and by the middle of the 1850s Americans were already at war on the Kansas and Missouri plains. Across the country, cities and towns were in various stages of revolt against federal authority. Fighting spread even further against Indians in the Far West and against Mormons in Utah. The nation's militants anticipated a coming breakdown, and worked to exploit it. John Brown, fresh from his actions in Kansas, moved east and planned more violence. Assembling a team from across the West, including black radicals from Oberlin, Ohio, and throughout communities in Canada West, Brown hatched a plan to attack Harper's Ferry, a federal weapon's arsenal in Virginia (now West Virginia). He would use the weapons to lead a slave revolt. Brown approached Frederick Douglass, though Douglass refused to join.

Brown's raid embarked on October 16. By October 18, a command under Robert E. Lee had crushed the revolt. [2] Five black men joined Brown's cause, including a former slave from Virginia named Dangerfield Newby who was the first man killed in the raid. Newby fought for the freedom of all slaves but particularly for the freedom of his wife, Harriet, and their children who remained enslaved in Prince William County, Virginia about fifty miles from Harper's Ferry. Discovered in Newby's

pocket following the raid were letters Harriet had written to him. In one from August 1859 she told her husband of the dread she felt at the possibility of her master selling her soon and her fervent desire to be reunited with him soon. [1]

I want you to buy me as soon as possible for if you do not get me somebody else will… it is said Master is in want of monney [sic] if so, I know not what time he may sell me an then all my bright hops [sic] of the futer [sic] are blasted for there has ben [sic] one bright hope to cheer me in all my troubles that is to be with you for if I thought I shoul [sic] never see you this earth would have no charms for me… (qtd. in Williams 51) [1]

Nine other of Brown's raiders were killed, including his own sons, were killed, but Brown himself lived and was imprisoned. Brown prophesied while in prison that the nation's crimes would only be purged with blood. He went to the gallows in December 1859. Northerners made a stunning display of sympathy on the day of his execution. Southerners took their reactions to mean that the coming 1860 election would be, in many ways, a referendum on secession and disunion. [1]

Republicans wanted little to do with Brown and instead tried to portray themselves as moderates opposed to both abolitionists and proslavery expansionists. In this climate, the parties opened their contest for the 1860 Presidential election. The Democratic Party fared poorly as its southern delegates bolted its national convention at Charleston and ran their own candidate, Vice President John C. Breckenridge of Kentucky. Hoping to field a candidate who might nonetheless manage to bridge the broken party's factions, the Democrats decided to meet again at Baltimore, and nominated Stephen A. Douglas of Illinois.

The Republicans, meanwhile, held their boisterous convention in Chicago. The Republican platform made the party's antislavery commitments clear, also making wide promises to its white constituents, particularly westerners, with the promise of new land, transcontinental railroads, and broad support of public schools. Abraham Lincoln, a candidate few outside of Illinois truly expected to win, nonetheless proved far less polarizing than the other names on the ballot. Lincoln won the nomination, and with the Democrats in disarray, Republicans knew their candidate Lincoln had a good chance of winning.

Abraham Lincoln won the 1860 contest on November 6, gaining just 40% of the popular vote and not a single southern vote in the Electoral College. Within days, southern states were organizing secession conventions. John J. Crittenden of Kentucky proposed a series of compromises, but a clear pro-southern bias meant they had little chance of gaining Republican acceptance. Crittenden's plan promised renewed enforcement of the Fugitive Slave Law and offered a plan to keep slavery in the nation's capital. Republicans by late 1860 knew that the voters who had just placed them in power did not want them to cave on these points, and southern states proceed with their plans to leave the Union. On December 20, South Carolina voted to secede, and issued its "Declaration of the Immediate Causes." The Declaration highlighted failure of the federal government to enforce the Fugitive Slave Act over competing personal liberty laws in northern states. After the war many southerners claimed that secession was primarily motivated by a concern to preserve states' rights, but the primary complaint of the very first ordinance of secession, listed the federal government's failure to exert its authority over the northern states.

The year 1861, then, saw the culmination of the secession crisis. Before he left for Washington, Lincoln told those who had gathered in Springfield to wish him well and that he faced a "task greater than Washington's" in the years to come. Southerners were also learning the challenges of forming a new nation. The seceded states grappled with internal divisions right away, as states with slaveholders sometimes did not support the newly seceded states. In January, for example, Delaware rejected secession. But states in the lower south adopted a different course. The State of Mississippi seceded. Later in the month, the states of Florida, Alabama, Georgia, and Louisiana also all left the Union. By early February, Texas had also joined the newly seceded states. In February, southerners drafted a constitution protecting slavery and named a westerner, Jefferson Davis of Mississippi, as their President. When Abraham Lincoln acted upon his constitutional mandate as Commander in Chief following his inauguration on March 4, rebels calling themselves members of the Confederate States of America opened fire on Fort Sumter in South Carolina. Within days, Abraham Lincoln would demand 75,000 volunteers from the North to crush the rebellion, and the American Civil War began. [2]

Conclusion

Slavery had long divided the politics of the United States. In time, these divisions became both sectional and irreconcilable. The first and most ominous sign of a coming sectional storm occurred over debates surrounding the admission of the State of Missouri in 1821. As westward expansion continued, these fault lines grew even more ominous, particularly as the United States managed to seize even more lands from its war with Mexico. The country seemed to teeter ever closer to a full-throated endorsement of slavery. But an antislavery coalition arose in the middle 1850s calling itself the Republican Party. Eager to

cordon off slavery and confine it to where it already existed, the Republicans won the presidential election of 1860 and threw the nation on the path to war.

Throughout this period, the mainstream of the antislavery movement remained committed to a peaceful resolution of the slavery issue through efforts understood to foster the "ultimate extinction" of slavery in due time. But as the secession crisis revealed, the South could not tolerate a federal government working against the interests of slavery's expansion and decided to take a gamble on war with the United States. Secession, in the end, raised the possibility of emancipation through war, a possibility most Republicans knew, of course, had always been an option, but one they nonetheless hoped would never be necessary. By 1861 all bets were off, and the fate of slavery, and of the nation, depended upon war. [2]

CC licensed content, Original

- **Authored by**: Florida State College at Jacksonville. **License**: *CC BY: Attribution*

CC licensed content, Shared previously

- The American YAWP. **Provided by**: Stanford University Press. **Located at**: http://www.americanyawp.com/index.html. **License**: *CC BY-SA: Attribution-ShareAlike*

CHAPTER OVERVIEW

9: AFRICAN AMERICANS AND THE CIVIL WAR

9.1: Introduction

African Americans and the Civil War

Module Introduction

When the Civil War began in April 1861, President Abraham Lincoln's paramount goal was the preservation of the union not the abolition of slavery. Though Lincoln detested slavery, viewed it as a moral sin, and believed it should not expand into new territories in the West, he, like many of his predecessors, hoped slavery would die a slow, natural death in the future. He regarded immediate abolition as too radical and unconstitutional. During the early years of the war, Lincoln also believed that any slaves freed as a consequence of the war, or by the volition of their masters, should be resettled outside of the United States. Not only did Lincoln not endorse abolition during the first year of the war, he did not believe freed black people could or should become citizens of the United States.

During the war, African-Americans—slave and free, in the North and South—forced President Lincoln to reconsider the meaning of the war. Black abolitionists like Frederick Douglass challenged Lincoln to fight not just the Confederate Army but the lifeblood of the Confederate states – their slave system. At the same time, slaves ran away from their masters into Union Army camps forcing the United States to develop policies that led to their emancipation during the war. Close to 200,000 black men, both former slaves and people born free, fought in all-black Union Army regiments during the war and distinguished themselves on and off the battlefield. Their bravery and commitment also eventually forced Lincoln to recognize the necessity of ensuring their freedom when the war ended as well as the freedom of all slaves.

Before his assassination in April 1865, Lincoln had dispensed with his proposal to colonize black people abroad and began to make provisional plans for Reconstruction that included extending voting rights to some black men, including Union Army veterans. African-Americans played a crucial role in shifting the meaning of the Civil War. Rather than a war simply about union, their actions made it into a war about emancipation, freedom, and citizenship. [1]

Learning Outcomes

This module addresses the following Course Learning Outcomes listed in the Syllabus for this course:

- To provide students with a general understanding of the history of African Americans within the context of American History.
- To motivate students to become interested and active in African American history by comparing current events with historical information.[1]

Additional learning outcomes associated with this module are:

- The student will be able to discuss the origins, evolution, and spread of racial slavery.
- The student will be able to describe the creation of a distinct African-American culture and how that culture became part of the broader American culture.
- The student will be able to describe how African-American, during times of war, have forced America to live up to its promise of freedom and equality [1]

Module Objectives

Upon completion of this module, the student will be able to:

Use primary historical documents to explain why and how African Americans fought to make the Civil War about freedom and emancipation. [1]

Readings and Resources

Learning Unit: African Americans and the Civil War (see below) [1]

CC licensed content, Original

- **Authored by**: Florida State College at Jacksonville. **License**: *CC BY: Attribution*

9.2: The Election of 1860 and Secession

African Americans and the Civil War

The Election of 1860 and Secession

The 1860 presidential election was chaotic. In April, the Democratic Party convened in Charleston, South Carolina, the bastion of secessionist thought in the South. The goal was to nominate a candidate for the party ticket, but the party was deeply divided. Northern Democrats pulled for Senator Stephen Douglas, a pro–slavery moderate championing popular sovereignty, while Southern Democrats were intent on endorsing someone other than Douglas. The parties leaders' refusal to include a pro–slavery platform resulted in Southern delegates walking out of the convention, preventing Douglas from gaining the two-thirds majority required for a nomination. The Democrats ended up with two presidential candidates. A subsequent convention in Baltimore nominated Douglas, while southerners nominated the current Vice President John C. Breckinridge of Kentucky as their presidential candidate. The nation's oldest party had split over differences in policy toward slavery.

Initially, the Republicans were hardly unified around a single candidate themselves. Several leading Republican men vied for their party's nomination. A consensus emerged at the May 1860 convention that the party's nominee would need to carry all the free states—for only in that situation could a Republican nominee potentially win. New York Senator William Seward, a leading contender, was passed over. Seward's pro–immigrant position posed a potential obstacle, particularly in Pennsylvania and New Jersey. Abraham Lincoln of Illinois, as a relatively unknown but likable politician, rose from a pool of potential candidates and was selected by the delegates on the third ballot. The electoral landscape was further complicated through the emergence of a fourth candidate, Tennessee's John Bell, heading the Constitutional Union Party. The Constitutional Unionists, comprised of former Whigs who teamed up with some southern Democrats, made it their mission to avoid the specter of secession while doing little else to address the issues tearing the country apart.

*A photograph taken in May/June 1864*Figure 9-1: African Americans collecting bones by John Reekie is in the Public Domain
.

Abraham Lincoln's nomination proved a great windfall for the Republican Party. Lincoln carried all free states with the exception of New Jersey (which he split with Douglas). 81.2% of the voting electorate came out to vote—at that point the highest ever for a presidential election. Lincoln received fewer than 40% of the popular vote, but with the field so split, that percentage yielded 180 electoral votes. Lincoln was trailed by Breckinridge with his 72 electoral votes, carrying 11 of the 15

slave states, Bell came in third with 39 electoral votes, and Douglas came in last, only able to garner twelve electoral votes despite carrying almost 30% of the popular vote. Since the Republican platform prohibited the expansion of slavery in future western states, all future Confederate states, with the exception of Virginia, excluded Lincoln's name from their ballots.

The election of Lincoln and the perceived threat to the institution of slavery proved too much for the deep Southern states. South Carolina acted almost immediately, calling a convention to declare secession. On December 20, 1860, the South Carolina convention voted unanimously 169–0 to dissolve their Union with the United States. The other states across the Deep South quickly followed suit. Mississippi adopted their own resolution on January 9, 1861, Florida followed on January 10, Alabama January 11, Georgia on January 19, Louisiana on January 26, and Texas on February 1. Texas was the only state to put the issue up for a popular vote, but secession was widely popular throughout the South.

Confederates quickly shed their American identity and adopted a new Confederate nationalism. Confederate nationalism was based on several ideals, foremost among these being slavery. As Confederate Vice President Alexander Stephens stated, the Confederacy's "foundations are laid, its cornerstone rests, upon the great truth that the negro is not equal to the white man; that slavery… is his natural and normal condition."

The election of Lincoln in 1860 demonstrated that the South was politically overwhelmed. Slavery was omnipresent in the pre-war South, and it served as the most common frame of reference for unequal power. To a Southern man, there was no fate more terrifying than the thought of being reduced to the level of a slave. Religion likewise shaped Confederate nationalism, as southerners believed that the Confederacy was fulfilling God's will. The Confederacy even veered from the American constitution by explicitly invoking Christianity in their founding document. Yet in every case, all rationale for secession could be thoroughly tied to slavery. "Our position is thoroughly identified with the institution of slavery– the greatest material interest of the world", proclaimed the Mississippi statement of secession. Thus for the original seven Confederate states (and those who would subsequently join), slavery's existence was the essential core of the fledging Confederacy.

A five dollar and a one-hundred-dollar Confederate States of America interest bearing banknote, c. 1861 and 1862. The emblems of nationalism on this currency reveal much about the ideology underpinning the Confederacy: George Washington standing stately in a Roman toga indicates the belief in the South's honorable and aristocratic past; John C. Calhoun's portrait emphasizes the Confederate argument of the importance of states' rights; and, most importantly, the image of African Americans working in fields demonstrates slavery's position as foundational to the Confederacy. [2]*Figure 9–2: Confederate 5 and 100 Dollar* by Confederate States of America is in the Public Domain .

Not all southerners participated in Confederate nationalism. Unionist southerners, most common in the upcountry where slavery was weakest, retained their loyalty to the Union. These southerners joined the Union army and worked to defeat the

Confederacy. Black southerners, most of whom were slaves, overwhelmingly supported the Union, often running away from plantations and forcing the Union army to reckon with slavery.

The seven seceding states met in Montgomery, Alabama on February 4th to organize a new nation. The delegates selected Jefferson Davis of Mississippi as president and established a capital in Montgomery, Alabama (it would move to Richmond in May). Whether other states of the Upper South would join the Confederacy remained uncertain. By the early spring of 1861, North Carolina and Tennessee had not held secession conventions, while voters in Virginia, Missouri, and Arkansas initially voted down secession. Despite this temporary boost to the Union, it became abundantly clear that these acts of loyalty in the Upper South were highly conditional and relied on a clear lack of intervention on the part of the Federal government. This was the precarious political situation facing Abraham Lincoln following his inauguration on March 4, 1861. [2]

9.3: A War for Union? (1861—1862)

A War for Union? (1861—1862)

In his inaugural address, Lincoln declared secession "legally void." While he did not intend to invade Southern states, he would use force to maintain possession of federal property within seceded states. Attention quickly shifted to the federal installation of Fort Sumter in Charleston, South Carolina. The fort was in need of supplies, and Lincoln intended to resupply it. South Carolina called for U.S. soldiers to evacuate the fort. Commanding officer Major Robert Anderson refused. On April 12, 1861, Confederate Brigadier General P. G. T. Beauregard fired on the fort. Anderson surrendered on April 13th and the Union troops evacuated. In response to the attack, President Abraham Lincoln called for 75,000 volunteers to serve three months to suppress the rebellion. The American Civil War had begun.

The assault on Fort Sumter and subsequent call for troops provoked several Upper South states to join the Confederacy. In total, eleven states renounced their allegiance to the United States. The new Confederate nation was predicated on the institution of slavery and the promotion of any and all interests that reinforced that objective. Some southerners couched their defense of slavery as a preservation of states' rights. But in order to protect slavery, the Confederate constitution left even less power to the states than the United States constitution, an irony not lost on many.

While Lincoln, his cabinet, and the War Department devised strategies to defeat the rebel insurrection, black Americans quickly forced the issue of slavery as a primary issue in the debate. As early as 1861, black Americans implored the Lincoln administration to serve in the army and navy. Lincoln initially waged a conservative, limited war. He believed that the presence of African American troops would threaten the loyalty of slaveholding border states, and white volunteers might refuse to serve alongside black men. However, army commanders could not ignore the growing populations of formerly enslaved people who escaped to freedom behind Union army lines. These former enslaved people took a proactive stance early in the war and forced the federal government to act. As the number of refugees ballooned, Lincoln and Congress found it harder to avoid the issue.

In May 1861, General Benjamin F. Butler went over his superiors' heads and began accepting fugitive slaves who came to Fortress Monroe in Virginia. In order to avoid the issue of the slaves' freedom, Butler reasoned that runaway slaves were "contraband of war," and he had as much a right to seize them as he did to seize enemy horses or cannons. Later that summer Congress affirmed Butler's policy in the First Confiscation Act. The act left "contrabands," as these runaways were called, in a state of limbo. Once a slave escaped to Union lines, her master's claim was nullified. She was not, however, a free citizen of the United States. Runaways lived in "contraband camps," where disease and malnutrition were rampant. Women and men were required to perform the drudgework of war: raising fortifications, cooking meals, and laying railroad tracks. Still, life as a contraband offered a potential path to freedom, and thousands of slaves seized the opportunity.

Fugitive slaves posed a dilemma for the Union military. Soldiers were forbidden to interfere with slavery or assist runaways, but many soldiers found such a policy unchristian. Even those indifferent to slavery were reluctant to turn away potential laborers or help the enemy by returning his property. Also, fugitive slaves could provide useful information on the local terrain and the movements of Confederate troops. Union officers became particularly reluctant to turn away fugitive slaves when Confederate commanders began forcing slaves to work on fortifications. Every slave who escaped to Union lines was a loss to the Confederate war effort. [2]

Runaway slaves fording the Rappahannock River in Virginia and into Union Army lines. Taken in August 1862. Figure 9–3:
Fugitive African Americans fording the Rappahannock by Timothy O'Sullivan is in the Public Domain .

The title of this political cartoon is "The (Fort) Monroe Doctrine. "Fort" is placed in parentheses, an allusion to President James Monroe's famous Monroe Doctrine, which prohibited European interference and colonialism in the Americas starting in 1823. [1] Figure 9–4: Fort Monroe doctrine cartoon by Unknown is in the Public Domain .

Despite the growing number of runaway slaves in Union Army camps, the Confederate Army won decisive battles against the Union during the summer of 1861, most notably at the Battle of Bull Run in July. The loss at Bull Run ruined Northern morale and destroyed any lingering hope that the war would be brief, relatively bloodless, and an inevitable Union victory. In response, Northern abolitionists, black and white, demanded that Republican congressmen, and the Lincoln Administration, make emancipation a primary war aim. "The result of [Bull Run] was a fearful blow," wrote one abolitionist, but "I think it may prove the means of rousing this stupid country to the extent & difficulty of the work it has to do." Frederick Douglass argued that a Confederate war for the defense of slavery must be met with a Union war for its destruction. [1]

To fight against slaveholders, without fighting against slavery, is but a half-hearted business, and paralyzes the hands engaged in it … Fire must be met with water…. War for the destruction of liberty must be met with the war for the destruction of slavery. (McPherson, "Battle Cry" 354) [1]

This decisive moment that prompted the issuance of the Emancipation Proclamation would occur in the fall of 1862 along Antietam creek in Maryland. Emboldened by their success in the previous spring and summer, Lee and Confederate President Jefferson Davis planned to win a decisive victory in Union territory and end the war. On September 17, 1862, McClellan and Lee's forces collided at the Battle of Antietam near the town of Sharpsburg. This battle was the first major battle of the Civil War to occur on Union soil. It remains the bloodiest single day in American history with over 20,000 soldiers killed, wounded, or missing in just twelve hours.

Soldiers killed on the battlefield at Antietam on September 17, 1862. Figure 9–5: Confederate dead by a fence on Hagerstown Road by Alexander Gardner is in the Public Domain .

Despite the Confederate withdrawal and the high death toll, the Battle of Antietam was not a decisive Union victory. It did, however, result in enough of a victory for Lincoln to issue the Emancipation Proclamation, which freed slaves in areas under Confederate control. There were significant exemptions to the Emancipation Proclamation including the border states, and parts of other states in the Confederacy. A far cry from a universal end to slavery, the Emancipation Proclamation nevertheless proved vital shifting the war aims from simple union to Emancipation. Framing it as a war measure, Lincoln and his Cabinet hoped that stripping the Confederacy of their labor force would not only debilitate the Southern economy, but also weaken Confederate morale. Furthermore, the Battle of Antietam and the issuance of the Emancipation Proclamation all but ensured that the Confederacy would not be recognized by European powers. Nevertheless, Confederates continued fighting. Union and Confederate forces clashed again at Fredericksburg, Virginia in December 1862. This Confederate victory resulted in staggering Union casualties.[2]

*A steel engraving from 1864.*Figure 9–6: Reading the Emancipation Proclamation by H.W. Herrick & J.W. Watts is in the Public Domain .

CC licensed content, Original

- **Authored by**: Florida State College at Jacksonville. **License**: *CC BY: Attribution*

CC licensed content, Shared previously

- The American YAWP. **Provided by**: Stanford University Press. **Located at**: http://www.americanyawp.com/index.html. **License**: *CC BY-SA: Attribution-ShareAlike*

Public domain content

- Fugitive African Americans fording the Rappahannock. **Authored by**: Timothy O'Sullivan. **Located at**: commons.wikimedia.org/wiki/File:Fugitive_African_Americans_fording_the_Rappahannock.jpg. **License**: *Public Domain: No Known Copyright*
- Fort Monroe doctrine cartoon. **Located at**: commons.wikimedia.org/wiki/File:Fort_monroe_doctrine_cartoon.jpg. **License**: *Public Domain: No Known Copyright*
- Confederate dead by a fence on Hagerstown Road. **Authored by**: Alexander Gardner. **Located at**: commons.wikimedia.org/wiki/File:Confederate_dead_by_a_fence_on_the_Hagerstown_road.png. **License**: *Public Domain: No Known Copyright*
- Reading the Emancipation Proclamation. **Authored by**: H.W. Herrick & J.W. Watts. **Located at**: commons.wikimedia.org/wiki/File:Reading_the_Emancipation_Proclamation_-_H.W._Herrick,_del.,_J.W._Watts,_sc._LCCN2003678043.jpg. **License**: *Public Domain: No Known Copyright*

9.4: War for Freedom (1863—1865)

War for Freedom (1863—1865)

As United States armies penetrated deeper into the Confederacy, politicians and the Union high command came to understand the necessity, and benefit, of enlisting black men in the army and navy. Although a few commanders began forming black units in 1862, such as Massachusetts abolitionist Thomas Wentworth Higginson's First South Carolina Volunteers (the Civil War's first black regiment), widespread enlistment did not occur until the Emancipation Proclamation went into effect on January 1, 1863. "And I further declare and make known," Lincoln's Proclamation read, "that such persons of suitable condition, will be received into the armed service of the United States to garrison forts, positions, stations, and other places, and to man vessels of all sorts in said service."

The language describing black enlistment indicated Lincoln's implicit desire to segregate African American troops from the main campaigning armies of white soldiers. "I believe it is a resource which, if vigorously applied now, will soon close the contest. It works doubly, weakening the enemy and strengthening us," Lincoln remarked in August 1863 about black soldiering. Although more than 180,000 black men (ten percent of the Union army) served during the war, the majority of United States Colored Troops (USCT) remained stationed behind the lines as garrison forces, often laboring and performing non–combat roles. [2]

When black soldiers did fight on the battlefield they distinguished themselves. Colonel Higginson, the white commander of the 1st South Carolina Volunteers, wrote a report about their valor and bravery following a skirmish along the South Carolina coast in January 1863 that was eventually published in Northern newspapers. "Nobody knows anything about these men who has not seen them in battle," Higginson wrote. "No officer in this regiment now doubts that the key to the successful prosecution of the war lies in the unlimited employment of black troops"

Soon thereafter, Governor John Andrew of Massachusetts received permission from the War Department to create an all-black regiment. Men enlisted in droves, which required creating two regiments, the 54th and 55th Massachusetts. (McPherson, "Battle Cry" 564–65) The 54th became one of the most recognized regiment's in the entire war. A 1989 film, Glory, starring Denzel Washington and Morgan Freeman, told a fictionalized version of the 54th's history and helped renew the regiment's renown in the twentieth century.

Figure 9–7: Company E, 4th U.S. Colored Infantry, at Fort Lincoln by William Morris Smith has no known copyright restrictions.

The courage and commitment of black soldiers did not, however, generate immediate enthusiasm or acceptance from white Northerners, including civilians and enlisted men. (McPherson, "Battle Cry" 565)

Black soldiers in the Union army endured rampant discrimination and earned less pay than white soldiers, while also facing the possibility of being murdered or sold into slavery if captured. James Henry Gooding, a black corporal in the famed 54th Massachusetts Volunteers, wrote to Abraham Lincoln in September 1863, questioning why he and his fellow volunteers were paid less than white men. Gooding argued that, because he and his brethren were born in the United States and selflessly left their private lives and to enter the army, they should be treated "as American SOLDIERS, not as menial hirelings." [2] In addition to protesting in letters to Lincoln, Secretary of War Edwin Stanton, and black run newspapers in the North such as Philadelphia's Christian Recorder, the soldiers of the 54th highlighted the injustice of unequal pay by refusing their paychecks while still fighting for their freedom and citizenship on the battlefield. [1]

African American soldiers defied the inequality of military service and used their positions in the army to reshape society, North and South. The majority of USCT (United States Colored Troops) had once been enslaved, and their presence as armed, blue-clad soldiers sent shockwaves throughout the Confederacy. To their friends and families, African American soldiers symbolized the embodiment of liberation and the destruction of slavery. To white southerners, they represented the utter disruption of the Old South's racial and social hierarchy. As members of armies of occupation, black soldiers wielded martial authority in towns and plantations. At the end of the war, as a black soldier marched by a cluster of Confederate prisoners, he noticed his former master among the group. "Hello, massa," the soldier exclaimed, "bottom rail on top dis time!"

The majority of USCT occupied the South by performing garrison duty, other black soldiers performed admirably on the battlefield, shattering white myths that docile, cowardly black men would fold in the maelstrom of war. Black troops fought in more than 400 battles and skirmishes, including Milliken's Bend and Port Hudson, Louisiana; Fort Wagner, South Carolina; Nashville; and the final campaigns to capture Richmond, Virginia. Fifteen black soldiers received the Medal of Honor, the highest honor bestowed for military heroism. Through their voluntarism, service, battlefield contributions, and even death,

black soldiers laid their claims for citizenship. "Once let a black man get upon his person the brass letters U.S." Frederick Douglass, the great black abolitionist, proclaimed, "and there is no power on earth which can deny that he has earned the right to citizenship."

Many slaves accompanied their masters in the Confederate army. They served their masters as "camp servants," cooking their meals, raising their tents, and carrying their supplies. The Confederacy also impressed slaves to perform manual labor. There are three important points to make about these "Confederate" slaves. First, their labor was almost always coerced. Second, people are complicated and have varying, often contradictory loyalties. A slave could hope in general that the Confederacy would lose but at the same time be concerned for the safety of his master and the Confederate soldiers he saw on a daily basis.

Finally, white Confederates did not see African Americans as their equals, much less as soldiers. There was never any doubt that black laborers and camp servants were property. Though historians disagree on the matter, it is a stretch to claim that not a single African American ever fired a gun for the Confederacy; a camp servant whose master died in battle might well pick up his dead master's gun and continue firing, if for no other reason than to protect himself. But this was always on an informal basis. The Confederate government did, in an act of desperation, pass a law in March 1865 allowing for the enlistment of black soldiers, but only a few dozen African Americans (mostly Richmond hospital workers) had enlisted by the war's end. [2]

In 1861, A.M. Chandler enlisted in the "Palo Alto Confederates," which became part of the 44th Mississippi Infantry Regiment. His mother, Louisa Gardner Chandler, sent Silas, one of her 36 slaves, with him. On September 20, 1863, the 44th Mississippi Infantry Regiment was engaged in the Battle of Chickamauga, where A.M. Chandler was wounded in his leg. A battlefield surgeon decided to amputate the leg but, according to the Chandler family, Silas accompanied him home to Mississippi where his leg was saved. His combat service ended as a result of the wound, but Silas returned to the war in January 1864 when A.M.'s younger brother, Benjamin, enlisted in the 9th Mississippi Cavalry Regiment [19]*Figure 9–8: Sergeant A.M. Chandler and Silas Chandler (family slave) by Library of Congress is in the* Public Domain *.*

The Draft Riots

An 1863 drawing that appeared in Harper's Weekly magazine titled, "Hanging a Negro, Clarkson Street." Figure 9–9: New York Draft Riots by Harper's Weekly is in the Public Domain .

By the end of the first week of July 1863, the North won significant, decisive battles against the South that seemed to turn the tide of the war. On July 3, after three days of brutal fighting, the Union Army finally defeated the Confederates led by General Robert E. Lee. The Union victory thwarted the Confederate invasion into the North and forced Lee and his troops to retreat back to Virginia. At the same time Union General Ulysses S. Grant finally wrested Vicksburg, Mississippi from Confederate forces and took control of the Mississippi River, effectively cutting the Confederacy in two.

Despite these advantages, Northern discontent over the war continued to grow, especially among portions of the white populace who did not favor fighting a bloody war for emancipation. This was particularly true in the wake of the Enrollment Act—the first effort at a draft among the northern populace during the Civil War. The working class citizens of New York felt especially angered as wealthy New Yorkers paid $300 for substitutes, sparing themselves from the hardships of war. "A rich man's war, but a poor man's fight," became a popular refrain. The Emancipation Proclamation convinced many immigrants in northern cities that freed people would soon take their jobs. This frustration culminated in the New York City Draft Riots in July 1863. Over the span of four days, the white populace killed some 120 citizens including the lynching of at least eleven black New Yorkers. Property damage was in the millions, including the complete destruction of more than fifty properties— most notably that of the Colored Orphan Asylum. In an ultimate irony, the largest civil disturbance to date in the United States (aside from the war itself) was only stopped by the deployment of Union soldiers, some of whom came directly from Gettysburg. [2]

9.5: Black Soldiers and Union War Victories (1864—1865)

Black Soldiers and Union War Victories (1864—1865)

Following the victory at Vicksburg, President Abraham Lincoln wrote to General Ulysses S. Grant, encouraging him to expand recruit of freed slaves into the Union Army. Lincoln now recognized that black soldiers were critical to eventual Union victory. He told Grant that they were "a resource which, if vigorously applied now, will soon close the contest. It works doubly, weakening the enemy and strengthening us." Grant agreed. He conveyed his "hearty support" for "arming the negro" to Lincoln.

This, with emancipation of the negro, is the heavyest [sic] blow yet given the Confederacy…. By arming the negro we have added a powerful ally.(McPherson, "Tried by War" 202)

In May of 1864 African American soldiers accompanied Union General William Tecumseh Sherman as he fought to take Atlanta, Georgia from Confederate forces and then began his march through the heart of Georgia and to the Atlantic coast where he captured Savannah and eventually Charleston, South Carolina in the winter of 1864 and 1865. Sherman and his troops burned and destroyed nearly everything in their path and freed thousands of slaves in the process. Further to the west, a black soldier from a Rhode Island regiment wrote about the fury he saw in the eyes of the white population of another occupied Southern city, New Orleans, Louisiana, when they saw black troops. At the same time, he expressed the pride he felt as he walked the streets of the occupied city:

In the city of New Orleans, we could see signs of smothered hate and prejudice to both our color and present character as Union soldiers. But, for once in his life, your humble correspondent walked fearlessly and boldly through the streets of a southern city! And he did this without being required to take off his cap at every step, or to give all the side–walks to those lordly princes of the sunny south, the planters' sons! (McPherson, "Negro's Civil War": 213–14; Carson et al. 226)

*Lincoln arriving in the abandoned Confederate capital of Richmond, Virginia.*Figure 9–10: President Lincoln Riding through Richmond, April 4, Amid the Enthusiastic Cheers of the Inhabitants by Library of Congress is in the Public Domain .

In early April 1865, the Confederacy was in its death throes. The President of the Confederate States of America, Jefferson Davis, evacuated Richmond, Virginia, the Confederate capital on Sunday, April 2 as Union forces approached. Two days later, President Abraham Lincoln walked through the streets of the vanquished city. Black slaves celebrated the arrival of the President and the Union army. Black Union soldiers, many of them former slaves, joined the slaves near a former slave auction site and jail. While the crowd listened to a black army chaplain preach a message of universal freedom, they suddenly heard

the shouts of imprisoned slaves who were left behind when the Confederates evacuated. The black soldiers released the men and women who praised God or "master Abe" as they walked the streets of Richmond as free people.(Davis, 298)[1]

Soon after Confederate General Robert E. Lee surrendered to Union General Ulysses S. Grant at Appomattox Court House, Virginia on April 9, 1865, black soldiers returned home in jubilation. In West Chester, Pennsylvania black soldiers rang the courthouse bell. In the New York, they led a parade. A black journalist from Philadelphia reported that, "The colored population was wild with enthusiasm. Old men thanked God in a very boisterous manner, and old women shouted upon the pavement as high as they ever had done at a religious revival." (Carson et al. 227–28)

Even before the war came to an official end African Americans envisioned a world without slavery, one in which they owned their own labor and land and determined their future. In January 1865, soon after the capture of Savannah, Georgia, Secretary of War Edwin Stanton traveled to the city to talk with General Sherman and local black leaders about how the Union Army could best support newly freed black families. "The way we can best take care of ourselves," they responded to Stanton, "is to have land, and turn in and till it by our labor.... We want to be placed on land until we are able to buy it, and make it our own." Sherman and Stanton agreed. Sherman responded by issuing his now infamous "Special Field Orders, No. 15," which set aside the Sea Islands along the Atlantic coast from Charleston south to Jacksonville, once the heart of the South's rice cotton growing region, for settlement by newly freed slaves. [1]

Under the order, each family could be given title to forty acres of land. Eventually, the Union Army settled some 40,000 free black people on lands once owned by white planters and slaveholders. The hope and promise offered by Sherman's order was short lived, however. Following Lincoln's assassination on April 14, 1865, less than a week after the war's conclusion, his Vice President Andrew Johnson, a conservative Democrat from Tennessee, became president. Johnson eventually revoked Sherman's order and restored the land rights of former Confederates by arguing that the lands had never been truly abandoned and legally seized. Therefore, Sherman's order, which was merely a war measure, could be overturned during peacetime. The dream of an independent black yeomanry living on lands where they once worked as slaves quickly faded. (McPherson, "Battle Cry" 841–42; Freehling 166; Weigley, 410; Carson et al, 227)

Freedom continued to bring African-Americans mixtures of joy and sorrow as they struggled to survive in a region devastated and impoverished in the aftermath of the war. They also faced hostility and resistance from whites who could not imagine or tolerate black freedom or even the suggestion of equality. "Nobody had his bearings," according to one former slave from Florida. Frank Bell, a black man from New Orleans, recalled how whites tried to reinstitute control and even ignore the legal abolition of slavery. His former master would not free him and told him, "Nigger, you's supposed to be free but I'll pay you a dollar a week and iffen you runs off I'll kill you." (Carson et al. 228)

To ensure the permanent legal end of slavery, Republicans drafted the Thirteenth Amendment during the war at President Lincoln's behest. [2]Lincoln's fervent desire to amend the Constitution in order to forever end slavery in the United States, something the Emancipation Proclamation could not do since it was only a war measure, was in many ways a result of the dedication and courage black soldiers displayed on the battlefield in 1863 and 1864. Lincoln received frequent pressure from conservative Northern Democrats to negotiate a peace to end the brutal war without guaranteeing the abolition of slavery. The president refused by pointing out the sacrifices made by black Union troops. "If they stake their lives for us they must be prompted by the strongest motive—even the promise of freedom. And the promise being made, must be kept." If he turned his back on these "black warriors," he said, he "should be damned in time & in eternity for so doing. The world shall know that I will keep my faith to friends & enemies, come what will." (Lincoln quoted in McPherson, "Battle Cry" 769) [1]

Yet the end of legal slavery did not mean the end of racial injustice. After the war, the Republican Reconstruction program of guaranteeing black rights succumbed to persistent racism and southern white violence. Long after 1865, most black southerners continued to labor on plantations, albeit as nominally free tenants or sharecroppers, while facing public segregation and voting discrimination. The effects of slavery endured long after emancipation. [2]

*This 1865 colored illustration celebrates the emancipation of slaves with the end of the Civil War. "Nast envisions a somewhat optimistic picture of the future of free blacks in the United States."*Figure 9–11: Emancipation by Th. Nast, King & Baird is in the Public Domain .

Conclusion

As battlefields fell silent in 1865, the question of secession had been answered, slavery had been eradicated, and America was once again territorially united. [2] African-Americans, North and Slave, slave and free, soldiers and civilians, had effectively forced President Abraham Lincoln, and the United States, to recognize emancipation and freedom as central to the military effort and meaning of the Civil War. As Lincoln said in his immortal Gettysburg Address on November 19, 1863 at the dedication of a Union cemetery there, "We here highly resolve that these dead shall not have died in vain—that this nation, under God, shall have a new birth of freedom—and that government of the people, by the people, for the people, shall not perish from the earth." (Lincoln, 1863) But the war's end brought questions about how to secure that freedom and construct a new bi–racial democracy. [1] Northern and southern soldiers returned home with broken bodies, broken spirits, and broken minds. Plantation owners had land but not labor. Recently freed African Americans had their labor but no land. Former slaves faced a world of possibilities–legal marriage, family reunions, employment, and fresh starts—but also a racist world of bitterness, violence, and limited opportunity. The war may have been over, but the battles for the peace were just beginning. [2]

CC licensed content, Original

- **Authored by**: Florida State College at Jacksonville. **License**: *CC BY: Attribution*

CC licensed content, Shared previously

- The American YAWP. **Provided by**: Stanford University Press. **Located at**: http://www.americanyawp.com/index.html. **License**: *CC BY-SA: Attribution-ShareAlike*

Public domain content

- President Lincoln Riding through Richmond, April 4, Amid the Enthusiastic Cheers of the Inhabitants. **Provided by**: Library of Congress. **Located at**: commons.wikimedia.org/wiki/File:President_Lincoln_riding_through_Richmond,_April_4,_amid_the_enthusiastic_cheers _of_the_inhabitants_LCCN99613987.tif. **License**: *Public Domain: No Known Copyright*
- Emancipation. **Authored by**: Th. Nast, King & Baird. **Located at**: commons.wikimedia.org/wiki/File:Emancipation_-_Th._Nast_;_King_%26_Baird,_printers,_607_Sansom_Street,_Philadelphia._LCCN2004665360.jpg. **License**: *Public Domain: No Known Copyright*

9.6: Primary Sources

Primary Source Document: Slaves—Thirty Years a Slave: From Bondage to Freedom by Louis Hughes

Document Download Link

Primary Source Document: Slaves—Selections from the WPA Interviews of Formerly Enslaved African Americans on Slavery

Document Download Link

Primary Source Document: Soldiers—Selections from the WPA Interviews of Formerly Enslaved African Americans on Being a Civil War Soldier.

Document Download Link

Primary Source Document: Soldiers—I Hope to Fall With My Face to the Foe by Lewis Douglas.

Document Download Link

Primary Source Document: Soldiers—Letters from Spotswood Rice.

Document Download Link

Primary Source Document: Soldiers—Letter to President Lincoln by Hannah Johnson

Document Download Link

Primary Source Document: Soldiers—Jacob Stroyer: My Experience in the Civil War

Document Download Link

Primary Source Document: Emancipation—Selections from the WPA Interviews of Formerly Enslaved African Americans on Emancipation

Document Download Link

Primary Source Document: Emancipation—Maryland Slave to the President

Document Download Link

Primary Source Document: Emancipation—George W. Hatton: Retaliation in Camp

Document Download Link

Primary Source Document: Emancipation—Black Residents of Nashville to the Union Convention

Document Download Link

See individual documents for correct attributions.

CC licensed content, Original

CHAPTER OVERVIEW

10: RECONSTRUCTION

10.1: Introduction

Reconstruction

Module Introduction

After the Civil War, much of the South lay in ruins. "It passes my comprehension to tell what became of our railroads," one South Carolinian told a Northern reporter. "We had passably good roads, on which we could reach almost any part of the State, and the next week they were all gone—not simply broken up, but gone. Some of the material was burned, I know, but miles and miles of iron have actually disappeared, gone out of existence." He might as well have been talking about the entire antebellum way of life. The future of the South was uncertain. How would these states be brought back into the Union? Would they be conquered territories or equal states? How would they rebuild their governments, economies, and social systems? What rights did freedom confer upon formerly enslaved people?

The answers to many of Reconstruction's questions hinged upon the concepts of citizenship and equality. The era witnessed perhaps the most open and widespread discussions of citizenship since the nation's founding. It was a moment of revolutionary possibility and violent backlash. African Americans and Radical Republicans pushed the nation to finally realize the Declaration of Independence&rsquo's promises that "all men were created equal" and had "certain, unalienable rights." White Democrats granted African Americans legal freedom but little more. When black Americans and their radical allies succeeded in securing citizenship for freedpeople, a new fight commenced to determine the legal, political, and social implications of American citizenship. Resistance continued, and Reconstruction eventually collapsed. In the South, limits on human freedom endured and would stand for nearly a century more. [2]

Learning Outcomes

This module addresses the following Course Learning Outcomes listed in the Syllabus for this course:

- To provide students with a general understanding of the history of African Americans within the context of American History.
- To motivate students to become interested and active in African American history by comparing current events with historical information.[1]

Additional learning outcomes associated with this module are:

- The student will be able to discuss the origins, evolution, and spread of racial slavery.
- The student will be able to describe the creation of a distinct African-American culture and how that culture became part of the broader American culture. [1]

Module Objectives

Upon completion of this module, the student will be able to:

- Analyze the long-term implications of Reconstruction for African Americans.
- Judge the legacy of the Reconstruction. [1]

Readings and Resources

Learning Unit: Reconstruction (see below) [1]

CC licensed content, Original

- **Authored by**: Florida State College at Jacksonville. **License**: *CC BY: Attribution*

CC licensed content, Shared previously

- The American YAWP. **Provided by**: Stanford University Press. **Located at**: http://www.americanyawp.com/index.html. **License**: *CC BY-SA: Attribution-ShareAlike*

10.2: Politics of Reconstruction

Reconstruction

Politics of Reconstruction

An 1862 photograph of former slaves from Virginia. Figure 10-1: *Cumberland Landing, Va. Group of 'contrabands' at Foller's house* by James F. Gibson is in the Public Domain .

Reconstruction—the effort to restore southern states to the Union and to redefine African Americans' place in American society—began before the Civil War ended. President Abraham Lincoln began planning for the reunification of the United States in the fall of 1863. With a sense that Union victory was imminent and that he could turn the tide of the war by stoking Unionist support in the Confederate states, Lincoln issued a proclamation allowing Southerners to take an oath of allegiance. When just ten percent of a state's voting population had taken such an oath, loyal Unionists could then establish governments. These so-called Lincoln governments sprang up in pockets where Union support existed like Louisiana, Tennessee, and Arkansas. Unsurprisingly, these were also the places that were exempted from the liberating effects of the Emancipation Proclamation.

Initially proposed as a war aim, Lincoln's Emancipation Proclamation committed the United States to the abolition of slavery. However, the Proclamation freed only slaves in areas of rebellion and left more than 700,000 in bondage in Delaware, Kentucky, Maryland, and Missouri as well as Union-occupied areas of Louisiana, Tennessee, and Virginia.

To cement the abolition of slavery, Congress passed the Thirteenth Amendment on January 31, 1865. The amendment and legally abolished slavery "except as a punishment for crime whereof the party shall have been duly convicted." Section Two of the amendment granted Congress the "power to enforce this article by appropriate legislation." State ratification followed, and by the end of the year the requisite three-fourths states had approved the amendment, and four million people were forever free from the slavery that had existed in North America for 250 years.

*An 1867 political drawing depicts newly enfranchised black men voting during Reconstruction.*Figure 10-2: *The First Vote* by Alfred R. Waud is in the Public Domain

Lincoln's policy was lenient, conservative, and short-lived. Reconstruction changed when John Wilkes Booth shot Lincoln on April 14, 1865, during a performance of "Our American Cousin" at the Ford Theater. Treated rapidly and with all possible care, Lincoln succumbed to his wounds the following morning, leaving a somber pall over the North and especially among African Americans.

The assassination of Abraham Lincoln propelled Vice President Andrew Johnson into the executive office in April 1865. Johnson, a states' rights, strict-constructionist and unapologetic racist from Tennessee, offered southern states a quick restoration into the Union. His Reconstruction plan required provisional southern governments to void their ordinances of secession, repudiate their Confederate debts, and ratify the Thirteenth Amendment. On all other matters, the conventions could do what they wanted with no federal interference. He pardoned all Southerners engaged in the rebellion with the exception of wealthy planters who possessed more than $20,000 in property. The southern aristocracy would have to appeal to Johnson for individual pardons. In the meantime, Johnson hoped that a new class of Southerners would replace the extremely wealthy in leadership positions.

Many southern governments enacted legislation that reestablished antebellum power relationships. South Carolina and Mississippi passed laws known as Black Codes to regulate black behavior and impose social and economic control. These laws granted some rights to African Americans, like the right to own property, to marry or to make contracts. But they also denied fundamental rights. White lawmakers forbade black men from serving on juries or in state militias, refused to recognize black testimony against white people, apprenticed orphan children to their former masters, and established severe vagrancy laws. Mississippi's vagrant law required all freedmen to carry papers proving they had means of employment. If they had no proof, they could be arrested and fined. If they could not pay the fine, the sheriff had the right to hire out his prisoner to anyone who was willing to pay the tax. Similar ambiguous vagrancy laws throughout the South reasserted control over black labor in what one scholar has called "slavery by another name." Black codes effectively criminalized black leisure, limited their mobility, and locked many into exploitative farming contracts. Attempts to restore the antebellum economic order largely succeeded.

These laws and outrageous mob violence against black southerners led Republicans to call for a more dramatic Reconstruction. So when Johnson announced that the southern states had been restored, congressional Republicans refused to seat delegates from the newly reconstructed states.

Republicans in Congress responded with a spate of legislation aimed at protecting freedmen and restructuring political relations in the South. Many Republicans were keen to grant voting rights for freed men in order to build a new powerful voting bloc. Some Republicans, like United States Congressman Thaddeus Stevens, believed in racial equality, but the majority were motivated primarily by the interest of their political party. The only way to protect Republican interests in the South was to give the vote to the hundreds of thousands of black men. Republicans in Congress responded to the codes with the Civil Rights Act of 1866, the first federal attempt to constitutionally define all American-born residents (except Native peoples) as citizens. The law also prohibited any curtailment of citizens' "fundamental rights."

The Fourteenth Amendment developed concurrently with the Civil Rights Act to ensure its constitutionality. The House of Representatives approved the Fourteenth Amendment on June 13, 1866. Section One granted citizenship and repealed the Taney Court's infamous Dred Scott (1857) decision. Moreover, it ensured that state laws could not deny due process or discriminate against particular groups of people. The Fourteenth Amendment signaled the federal government's willingness to enforce the Bill of Rights over the authority of the states.

Based on his belief that African Americans did not deserve rights, President Johnson opposed both the passage of the Fourteenth Amendment and vetoed the Civil Rights Act, as he believed black Americans did not deserve citizenship. With a two-thirds majority gained in the 1866 midterm elections, Republicans overrode the veto, and in 1867, they passed the first of two Reconstruction Acts, which dissolved state governments and divided the South into five military districts. Before states could rejoin the Union, they would have to ratify the Fourteenth Amendment, write new constitutions enfranchising African Americans, and abolish black codes. The Fourteenth Amendment was finally ratified on July 9, 1868.

*The first African American Senator and members of the House of Representatives in Washington, D.C.*Figure 10-3: *First Colored Senator and Representatives* by Currier and Ives is in the Public Domain .

In the 1868 Presidential election, former Union General Ulysses S. Grant ran on a platform that proclaimed, "Let Us Have Peace" in which he promised to protect the new status quo. On the other hand, the Democratic candidate, Horatio Seymour, promised to repeal Reconstruction. Black Southern voters helped Grant him win most of the former Confederacy.

Reconstruction brought the first moment of mass democratic participation for African Americans. In 1860, only five states in the North allowed African Americans to vote on equal terms with whites. Yet after 1867, when Congress ordered Southern states to eliminate racial discrimination in voting, African Americans began to win elections across the South. In a short time, the South was transformed from an all-white, pro-slavery, Democratic stronghold to a collection of Republican-led states with African Americans in positions of power for the first time in American history.

Through the provisions of the Congressional Reconstruction Acts, black men voted in large numbers and also served as delegates to the state constitutional conventions in 1868. Black delegates actively participated in revising state constitutions. One of the most significant accomplishments of these conventions was the establishment of a public school system. While public schools were virtually nonexistent in the antebellum period, by the end of Reconstruction, every Southern state had established a public school system. Republican officials opened state institutions like mental asylums, hospitals, orphanages, and prisons to white and black residents, though often on a segregated basis. They actively sought industrial development, northern investment, and internal improvements.

African Americans served at every level of government during Reconstruction. At the federal level, Hiram Revels and Blanche K. Bruce were chosen as United States Senators from Mississippi. Fourteen men served in the House of Representatives. At least two hundred seventy other African American men served in patronage positions as postmasters, customs officials, assessors, and ambassadors. At the state level, more than 1,000 African American men held offices in the South. P. B. S. Pinchback served as Louisiana's Governor for thirty-four days after the previous governor was suspended during impeachment proceedings and was the only African American state governor until Virginia elected L. Douglass Wilder in 1989. Almost 800 African American men served as state legislators around the South with African Americans at one time making up a majority in the South Carolina House of Representatives.

African American office holders came from diverse backgrounds. Many had been born free or had gained their freedom before the Civil War. Many free African Americans, particularly those in South Carolina, Virginia, and Louisiana, were wealthy and well educated, two facts that distinguished them from much of the white population both before and after the Civil War. Some like Antione Dubuclet of Louisiana and William Breedlove from Virginia owned slaves before the Civil War. Others had helped slaves escape or taught them to read like Georgia's James D. Porter.

The majority of African American office holders, however, gained their freedom during the war. Among them were skilled craftsman like Emanuel Fortune, a shoemaker from Florida, minsters such as James D. Lynch from Mississippi, and teachers like William V. Turner from Alabama. Moving into political office was a natural continuation of the leadership roles they had held in their former slave communities.

By the end of Reconstruction in 1877, more than 2,000 African American men had served in offices ranging from mundane positions such as local Levee Commissioner to United States Senator. When the end of Reconstruction returned white Democrats to power in the South, all but a few African American office holders lost their positions. After Reconstruction, African Americans did not enter the political arena again in large numbers until well into the twentieth century. [2]

The Meaning of Black Freedom

*An 1862 photograph showing a family of former slaves on a South Carolina plantation.*Figure 10-4: *Family of African American slaves on Smith's Plantation Beaufort South Carolina* by Timothy O'Sullivan is in the Public Domain .

In an 1866 sketch, black women learning a trade (sewing) in a school run by the Freedmen's Bureau in Richmond, Virginia during Reconstruction. Figure 10-5: *Glimpses at the Freedmen* by Jas. E. Taylor is in the Public Domain .

A photograph from the late nineteenth century of African-American church members in Georgia standing in front of their church. Figure 10-6: *African Americans standing outside of a church* by unknown photographer and prepared by W. E. B. DuBois is in the Public Domain .

Land was one of the major desires of the freed people. Frustrated by responsibility for the growing numbers of freed people following his troops, General William T. Sherman issued Special Field Order No. 15 in which land in Georgia and South Carolina was to be set aside as a homestead for the freedpeople. Sherman lacked the authority to confiscate and distribute land, so this plan never fully took effect. One of the main purposes of the Freedmen's Bureau, however, was to redistribute lands to former slaves that had been abandoned and confiscated by the federal government. Even these land grants were short lived. In 1866, land that ex-Confederates had left behind was reinstated to them.

Freedpeople's hopes of land reform were unceremoniously dashed as Freedmen's Bureau agents held meetings with the freedmen throughout the South, telling them the promise of land was not going to be honored and that instead they should plan to go back to work for their former owners as wage laborers. The policy reversal came as quite a shock. In one instance, Freedmen's Bureau Commissioner General Oliver O. Howard went to Edisto Island to inform the black population there of the policy change. The black commission's response was that "we were promised Homesteads by the government… You ask us to forgive the land owners of our island…The man who tied me to a tree and gave me 39 lashes and who stripped and flogged my mother and my sister… that man I cannot well forgive. Does it look as if he has forgiven me, seeing how he tries to keep me in a condition of helplessness?"

In working to ensure that crops would be harvested, agents sometimes coerced former slaves into signing contracts with their former masters. However, the Bureau also instituted courts where African Americans could seek redress if their employers

were abusing them or not paying them. The last ember of hope for land redistribution was extinguished when Thaddeus Stevens and Charles Sumner's proposed land reform bills were tabled in Congress. Radicalism had its limits, and the Republican Party's commitment to economic stability eclipsed their interest in racial justice.

Another aspect of the pursuit of freedom was the reconstitution of families. Many freedpeople immediately left plantations in search of family members who had been sold away. Newspaper ads sought information about long lost relatives. People placed these ads until the turn of the 20 [th]century, demonstrating the enduring pursuit of family reunification. Freedpeople sought to gain control over their own children or other children who had been apprenticed to white masters either during the war or as a result of the Black Codes. Above all, freedpeople wanted freedom to control their families.

Many freedpeople rushed to solemnize unions with formal wedding ceremonies. Black people's desires to marry fit the government's goal to make free black men responsible for their own households and to prevent black women and children from becoming dependent on the government.

Freedpeople placed a great emphasis on education for their children and themselves. For many, the ability to finally read the Bible for themselves induced work-weary men and women to spend all evening or Sunday attending night school or Sunday school classes. It was not uncommon to find a one-room school with more than 50 students ranging in age from 3 to 80. As Booker T. Washington famously described the situation, "it was a whole race trying to go to school. Few were too young, and none too old, to make the attempt to learn."

Many churches served as schoolhouses and as a result became central to the freedom struggle. Free and freed black southerners carried well-formed political and organizational skills into freedom. They developed anti-racist politics and organizational skills through anti-slavery organizations turned church associations. Liberated from white-controlled churches, black Americans remade their religious worlds according to their own social and spiritual desires.

One of the more marked transformations that took place after emancipation was the proliferation of independent black churches and church associations. In the 1930s, nearly 40% of 663 black churches surveyed had their organizational roots in the post-emancipation era. Many independent black churches emerged in the rural areas and most of them had never been affiliated with white churches.

Many of these independent churches were quickly organized into regional, state, and even national associations, often by brigades of northern and midwestern free blacks who went to the South to help the freedmen. Through associations like the Virginia Baptist State Convention and the Consolidated American Baptist Missionary Convention, Baptists became the fastest growing post-emancipation denomination, building on their anti-slavery associational roots and carrying on the struggle for black political participation.

Tensions between Northerners and Southerners over styles of worship and educational requirements strained these associations. Southern, rural black churches preferred worship services with more emphasis on inspired preaching, while northern urban blacks favored more orderly worship and an educated ministry.

Perhaps the most significant internal transformation in churches had to do with the role of women—a situation that eventually would lead to the development of independent women's conventions in Baptist, Methodist and Pentecostal churches. Women like Nannie Helen Burroughs and Virginia Broughton, leaders of the Baptist Woman's Convention, worked to protect black women from sexual violence from white men. Black representatives repeatedly articulated this concern in state constitutional conventions early in the Reconstruction era. In churches, women continued to fight for equal treatment and access to the pulpit as preachers, even though they were able to vote in church meetings.

Black churches provided centralized leadership and organization in post-emancipation communities. Many political leaders and officeholders were ministers. Churches were often the largest building in town and served as community centers. Access to pulpits and growing congregations, provided a foundation for ministers' political leadership. Groups like the Union League, militias and fraternal organizations all used the regalia, ritual and even hymns of churches to inform and shape their practice.

Black Churches provided space for conflict over gender roles, cultural values, practices, norms, and political engagement. With the rise of Jim Crow, black churches would enter a new phase of negotiating relationships within the community and the wider world. [2]

Reconstruction and Women

Reconstruction involved more than the meaning of emancipation. Women also sought to redefine their roles within the nation and in their local communities. The abolitionist and women's rights movements simultaneously converged and began to clash. In the South, both black and white women struggled to make sense of a world of death and change. In Reconstruction, leading women's rights advocate Elizabeth Cady Stanton saw an unprecedented opportunity for disenfranchised groups. Women as well as black Americans, North and South could seize political rights. Stanton formed the Women's Loyal National League in 1863, which petitioned Congress for a constitutional amendment abolishing slavery. The Thirteenth Amendment marked a victory not only for the antislavery cause, but also for the Loyal League, proving women's political efficacy and the possibility for radical change. Now, as Congress debated the meanings of freedom, equality, and citizenship for former slaves, women's rights leaders saw an opening to advance transformations in women's status, too. On the tenth of May 1866, just one year after the war, the Eleventh National Women's Rights Convention met in New York City to discuss what many agreed was an extraordinary moment, full of promise for fundamental social change. Elizabeth Cady Stanton presided over the meeting. Also in attendance were prominent abolitionists with whom Stanton and other women's rights leaders had joined forces in the years leading up to the war. Addressing this crowd of social reformers, Stanton captured the radical spirit of the hour: "now in the reconstruction," she declared, "is the opportunity, perhaps for the century, to base our government on the broad principle of equal rights for all." Stanton chose her universal language—"equal rights for all"—with intention, setting an agenda of universal suffrage. Thus, in 1866, the National Women's Rights Convention officially merged with the American Antislavery Society to form the American Equal Rights Association (AERA). This union marked the culmination of the longstanding partnership between abolitionist and women's rights advocates.

The AERA was split over whether black male suffrage should take precedence over universal suffrage, given the political climate of the South. Some worried that political support for freedmen would be undermined by the pursuit of women's suffrage. For example, AERA member Frederick Douglass insisted that the ballot was literally a "question of life and death" for southern black men, but not for women. Some African-American women challenged white suffrists in other ways. Frances Harper, for example, a free-born black woman living in Ohio, urged them to consider their own privilege as white and middle class. Universal suffrage, she argued, would not so clearly address the complex difficulties posed by racial, economic, and gender inequality.

These divisions came to a head early in 1867, as the AERA organized a campaign in Kansas to determine the fate of black and woman suffrage. Elizabeth Cady Stanton and her partner in the movement, Susan B. Anthony, made the journey to advocate universal suffrage. Yet they soon realized that their allies were distancing themselves from women's suffrage in order to advance black enfranchisement. Disheartened, Stanton and Anthony allied instead with white supremacists that supported women's equality. Many fellow activists were dismayed by Stanton and Anthony's willingness to appeal to racism to advance their cause.

These tensions finally erupted over conflicting views of the Fourteenth and Fifteenth Amendments. Women's rights leaders vigorously protested the Fourteenth Amendment. Although it established national citizenship for all persons born or naturalized in the United States, the amendment also introduced the word "male" into the Constitution for the first time. After the Fifteenth Amendment ignored "sex" as an unlawful barrier to suffrage, an omission that appalled Stanton, the AERA officially dissolved. Stanton and Anthony formed the National Woman Suffrage Association (NWSA), while those suffrists who supported the Fifteenth Amendment, regardless of its limitations, founded the American Woman Suffrage Association (AWSA).

The NWSA soon rallied around a new strategy: the 'New Departure'. This new approach interpreted the Constitution as already guaranteeing women the right to vote. They argued that by nationalizing citizenship for all persons, and protecting all rights of citizens—including the right to vote—the Fourteenth and Fifteenth Amendments guaranteed women's suffrage.

Broadcasting the New Departure, the NWSA encouraged women to register to vote, which roughly seven hundred did between 1868 and 1872. Susan B. Anthony was one of them and was arrested but then acquitted in trial. In 1875, the Supreme Court addressed this constitutional argument: acknowledging women's citizenship, but arguing that suffrage was not a right guaranteed to all citizens. This ruling not only defeated the New Departure, but also coincided with the Court's broader reactionary interpretation of the Reconstruction Amendments that significantly limited freedmen's rights. Following this defeat, many suffrists like Stanton increasingly replaced the ideal of 'universal suffrage' with arguments about the virtue that white women would bring to the polls. These new arguments often hinged on racism and declared the necessity of white women voters to keep black men in check.

Advocates for women's suffrage were largely confined to the North, but southern women were experiencing social transformations as well. The lines between refined white womanhood and degraded enslaved black femaleness were no longer so clearly defined. Moreover, during the war, southern white women had been called upon to do traditional man's work, chopping wood and managing businesses. While white southern women decided whether and how to return to their prior status, African American women embraced new freedoms and a redefinition of womanhood.

Southern black women sought to redefine their public and private lives. Their efforts to control their labor met the immediate opposition of southern white women. Gertrude Clanton, a plantation mistress before the war, disliked cooking and washing dishes, so she hired an African American woman to do the washing. A misunderstanding quickly developed. The laundress, nameless in Gertrude's records, performed her job and returned home. Gertrude believed that her money had purchased a day's labor, not just the load of washing, and she became quite frustrated. Meanwhile, this washerwoman and others like her set wages and hours for themselves, and in many cases began to take washing into their own homes in order to avoid the surveillance of white women and the sexual threat posed by white men.

Similar conflicts raged across the South. White Southerners demanded that African American women work in the plantation home and instituted apprenticeship systems to place African American children in unpaid labor positions. African American women combated these attempts by refusing to work at jobs without fair pay or fair conditions and by clinging tightly to their children.

African American women formed clubs to bury their dead, to celebrate African American masculinity, and to provide aid to their communities. On May 1, 1865, African Americans in Charleston created the precursor to the modern Memorial Day by mourning the Union dead buried hastily on a race track-turned prison. Like their white counterparts, the 300 African American women who participated had been members of the local Patriotic Association, which aided freed people during the war. African American women continued participating in Federal Decoration Day ceremonies and, later, formed their own club organizations. Racial violence, whether city riots or rural vigilantes, continued to threaten these vulnerable households. Nevertheless, the formation and preservation of African American households became a paramount goal for African American women. [2]

10.3: Racial Violence in Reconstruction

Racial Violence in Reconstruction

Violence shattered the dream of biracial democracy. Still steeped in the violence of slavery, white Southerners could scarcely imagine black free labor. Congressional investigator, Carl Schurz, reported that in the summer of 1865, Southerners shared a near unanimous sentiment that "You cannot make the negro work, without physical compulsion." Violence had been used in the antebellum period to enforce slave labor and to define racial difference. In the post-emancipation period it was used to stifle black advancement and return to the old order.

Much of life in the antebellum South had been premised on slavery. The social order rested upon a subjugated underclass, and the labor system required unfree laborers. A notion of white supremacy and black inferiority undergirded it all. Whites were understood as fit for freedom and citizenship, blacks for chattel slave labor. The Confederate surrender at Appomattox Court House and the subsequent adoption by the U.S. Congress of the Thirteenth Amendment destroyed the institution of American slavery and threw the southern society into disarray. The foundation of southern society had been shaken, but southern whites used black codes and racial terrorism to reassert control of former slaves.

Figure 10-7: *Visit of the Ku-Klux* by Frank Bellew is in the Public Domain .

Racial violence in the Reconstruction period took three major forms: riots against black political authority, interpersonal fights, and organized vigilante groups. There were riots in southern cities several times during Reconstruction. The most notable were the riots in Memphis and New Orleans in 1866, but other large-scale urban conflicts erupted in places including Laurens, South Carolina in 1870; Colfax, Louisiana in 1873; another in New Orleans in 1874; Yazoo City, Mississippi in 1875; and Hamburg, South Carolina in 1876. Southern cities grew rapidly after the war as migrants from the countryside—particularly freed slaves—flocked to urban centers. Cities became centers of Republican control. But white conservatives chafed at the influx of black residents and the establishment of biracial politics. In nearly every conflict, white conservatives initiated

violence in reaction to Republican rallies or conventions or elections in which black men were to vote. The death tolls of these conflicts remain incalculable, and victims were overwhelmingly black.

Figure 10-8: *The Union as It Was* by Thomas Nast is in the Public Domain .

Even everyday violence between individuals disproportionally targeted African Americans during Reconstruction. African Americans gained citizenship rights like the ability to serve on juries as a result of the Civil Rights Act of 1866 and the Fourteenth Amendment. But southern white men were almost never prosecuted for violence against black victims. White men beat or shot black men with relative impunity, and did so over minor squabbles, labor disputes, longstanding grudges, and crimes of passion. These incidents sometimes were reported to local federal authorities like the army or the Freedmen's Bureau, but more often than not such violence was unreported and unprosecuted.

The violence committed by organized vigilante groups, sometimes called nightriders or bushwhackers was more often premeditated. Groups of nightriders operated under cover of darkness and wore disguises to curtail black political involvement. Nightriders harassed and killed black candidates and office holders and frightened voters away from the polls. They also aimed to limit black economic mobility by terrorizing freedpeople who tried to purchase land or otherwise become too independent from the white masters they used to rely on. They were terrorists and vigilantes, determined to stop the erosion of the antebellum South, and they were widespread and numerous, operating throughout the South. The Ku Klux Klan emerged in the late 1860s as the most infamous of these groups.

The Ku Klux Klan was organized in 1866 in Pulaski, Tennessee and had spread to nearly every state of the former Confederacy by 1868. The Klan drew heavily from the antebellum southern elite, but Klan groups sometimes overlapped with criminal gangs or former Confederate guerilla groups. The Klan's reputation became so potent, and its violence so widespread, that many groups not formally associated with it were called Ku Kluxers, and to "Ku Klux" meant to commit vigilante violence. While it is difficult to differentiate Klan actions from those of similar groups, such as the White Line, Knights of the White Camellia, and the White Brotherhood, the distinctions hardly matter. All such groups were part of a web of terror that spread throughout the South during Reconstruction. In Panola County, Mississippi, between August 1870 and December 1872, twenty-four Klan-style murders occurred. And nearby, in Lafayette County, Klansmen drowned thirty black Mississippians in a single mass murder. Sometimes the violence was aimed at "uppity" black men or women who had tried to buy land or dared to be insolent toward a white southerner. Other times, as with the beating of Republican sheriff and tax collector Allen Huggins, the Klan targeted white politicians who supported freedpeople's civil rights. Numerous, perhaps dozens, of Republican politicians were killed, either while in office or while campaigning. Thousands of individual citizens, men and women, white and black, had their homes raided and were whipped, raped, or murdered.

1872 drawing of the Ku Klux Klan members from Tishamingo County, Mississippi. Figure 10-9: *Mississippi ku klux klan* by Unknown is in the Public Domain .

The federal government responded to southern paramilitary tactics by passing the Enforcement Acts between 1870 and 1871. The acts made it criminal to deprive African Americans of their civil rights. The acts also deemed violent Klan behavior as acts of rebellion against the United States and allowed for the use of U.S. troops to protect freedpeople. For a time, the federal government, its courts, and its troops, sought to put an end to the KKK and related groups. But the violence continued. By 1876, as southern Democrats reestablished "home rule" and "redeemed" the South from Republicans, federal opposition to the KKK weakened. National attention shifted away from the South and the activities of the Klan, but African Americans remained trapped in a world of white supremacy that restricted their economic, social, and political rights.

White conservatives would assert that Republicans, in denouncing violence, were "waving a bloody shirt" for political opportunity. The violence, according to many white conservatives, was fabricated, or not as bad as it was claimed, or an unavoidable consequence of the enfranchisement of African Americans. On December 22, 1871, R. Latham of Yorkville, South Carolina wrote to the *New York Tribune* , voicing the beliefs of many white Southerners as he declared that "the same principle that prompted the white men at Boston, disguised as Indians, to board, during the darkness of night, a vessel with tea, and throw her cargo into the Bay, clothed some of our people in Ku Klux gowns, and sent them out on missions technically illegal. Did the Ku Klux do wrong? You are ready to say they did and we will not argue the point with you... Under the peculiar circumstances what could the people of South Carolina do but resort to Ku Kluxing?"

Victims and witnesses to the violence told a different story. Sallie Adkins of Warren County, Georgia, was traveling with her husband, Joseph, a Georgia state senator, when he was assassinated by Klansmen on May 10, 1869. She wrote President Ulysses S. Grant, asking for both physical protection and justice. "I am no Statesman," she disclaimed, "I am only a poor woman whose husband has been murdered for his devotion to his country. I may have very foolish ideas of Government, States & Constitutions. But I feel that I have claims upon my country. The Rebels imprisoned my Husband. Pardoned Rebels murdered him. There is no law for the punishment of them who do deeds of this sort... I demand that you, President Grant, keep the pledge you made the nation—make it safe for any man to utter boldly and openly his devotion to the United States."

The political and social consequences of the violence were as lasting as the physical and mental trauma suffered by victims and witnesses. Terrorism worked to end federal involvement in Reconstruction and helped to usher in a new era of racial repression.

*An early 1900s photograph from Florida.*Figure 10-10: *A Southern Chain Gang* by Detroit Publishing Co. has no known copyright restrictions.

African Americans actively sought ways to shed the vestiges of slavery. Many discarded the names their former masters had chosen for them and adopted new names like "Freeman" and "Lincoln" that affirmed their new identities as free citizens. Others resettled far from their former plantations, hoping to eventually farm their own land or run their own businesses. By the end of Reconstruction, the desire for self-definition, economic independence, and racial pride coalesced in the founding of dozens of black towns across the South. Perhaps the most well-known of these towns was Mound Bayou, Mississippi, a Delta town established in 1887 by Isaiah Montgomery and Ben Green, former slaves of Joseph and Jefferson Davis. Residents of the town took pride in the fact that African Americans owned all of the property in town, including banks, insurance companies, shops, and the surrounding farms. The town celebrated African American cultural and economic achievements during their annual festival, Mound Bayou Days. These tight-knit communities provided African Americans with spaces where they could live free from the indignities of segregation and the exploitation of sharecropping on white-owned plantations.

Freedom also empowered African Americans in the South to rebuild families, make contracts, hold property and move freely for the first time. Republican's in the South attempted to transform the region into a free-labor economy like the North. Yet the transition from slave labor to free labor was never so clear. Well into the twentieth century, white Southerners used a combination of legal force and extra-legal violence to maintain systems of bound labor. Vagrancy laws enabled law enforcement to justify arrest of innocent black men and women, and the convict-lease system meant that even an arbitrary arrest could result in decades of forced, uncompensated labor. This new form of slavery continued until World War II.

Re-enslavement was only the most extreme example of an array of economic injustices. In the later nineteenth-century, poor whites would form mobs and go "white-capping" to scare away black job-seekers. Lacking the means to buy their own farms, black famers often turned to sharecropping. Sharecropping often led to cycles of debt that kept families bound to the land. (2)

- THE UNION AS IT WAS. **Authored** **by:** Thomas Nast. **Located** **at:** commons.wikimedia.org/wiki/File:The_Union_as_It_Was.jpg. **License:** *Public Domain: No Known Copyright*
- MISSISSIPPI KU KLUX KLAN. **Located** **at:** commons.wikimedia.org/wiki/File:Mississippi_ku_klux.jpg. **License:** *Public Domain: No Known Copyright*
- A SOUTHERN CHAIN GANG. **Provided** **by:** Detroit Publishing Co.. **Located** **at:** commons.wikimedia.org/wiki/File:A_Southern_chain_gang_c1903-restore.jpg. **License:** *Public Domain: No Known Copyright*

10.4: The End of Reconstruction

The End of Reconstruction

Reconstruction concluded when national attention turned away from the integration of former slaves as equal citizens. White Democrats recaptured southern politics. Between 1868 and 1877, and accelerating after the Depression of 1873, national interest in Reconstruction dwindled as economic issues moved to the foreground. The biggest threat to Republican power in the South was violence and intimidation by white conservatives, staved off by the presence of federal troops in key southern cities. But the United States never committed the manpower required to restore order, if such a task was even possible. Reconstruction finally ended with the contested Presidential election of 1876. Republican Rutherford B. Hayes was given the presidency in exchange for the withdrawal of federal troops from the South. But by 1876, the vast majority of federal troops had already left.

Republicans and Democrats responded to the economic declines by shifting attention from Reconstruction to economic recovery. War weary from nearly a decade of bloody military and political strife, so-called Stalwart Republicans turned from idealism, focusing their efforts on economics and party politics. They grew to particular influence during Ulysses S. Grant's first term (1868-1872). After the death of Thaddeus Stevens in 1868 and the political alienation of Charles Sumner by 1870, Stalwart Republicans assumed primacy in Republican Party politics, putting Reconstruction on the defensive within the very party leading it.

Meanwhile, New Departure Democrats gained strength by distancing themselves from pro-slavery Democrats and Copperheads. They focused on business, economics, political corruption, and trade, instead of Reconstruction. In the South, New Departure Democrats were called Redeemers, and were initially opposed by Southerners who clung tightly to white supremacy and the Confederacy. But between 1869 and 1871, their home rule platform, asserting that good government was run by locals—meaning white Democrats, rather than black or white Republicans—helped end Reconstruction in three important states: Tennessee, Virginia, and Georgia.

In September 1873, Jay Cooke and Company declared bankruptcy, resulting in a bank run that spiraled into a six-year depression. The Depression of 1873 destroyed the nation's fledgling labor movement and helped quell northerners' remaining idealism about Reconstruction. In the South, many farms were capitalized entirely through loans. After 1873, most sources of credit vanished, forcing many landowners to default, driving them into an over-saturated labor market. Wages plummeted, contributing to the growing system of debt peonage in the South that trapped workers in endless cycles of poverty. The economic turmoil enabled the Democrats to take control of the House of Representatives after the 1874 elections.

On the eve of the 1876 Presidential election, the nation still reeled from depression. The Grant administration found itself no longer able to intervene in the South due to growing national hostility to interference in southern affairs. Scandalous corruption in the Grant Administration had sapped the national trust. By 1875, Democrats in Mississippi hatched the Mississippi Plan, a wave of violence designed to suppress black voters. The state's Republican governor urged federal involvement, but national Republicans ignored the plea.

Meanwhile, the Republican candidate for governor of Ohio, Rutherford B. Hayes, won big without mentioning Reconstruction, focusing instead on avoiding corruption, recovering the economy, and discouraging alcohol use. His success entered him into the running as a potential Presidential candidate. The stage was set for an election that would end Reconstruction as a national issue.

Republicans chose Rutherford B. Hayes as their nominee while Democrats chose Samuel J. Tilden, who ran on honest politics and home rule in the South. Allegations of voter fraud and intimidation emerged in the three states where Reconstruction held strong. Florida, Louisiana, and South Carolina would determine the president. Indeed, those elections were fraught with violence and fraud because of the impunity with which white conservatives felt they could operate in detering Republican voters. A special electoral commission voted along party lines—eight Republicans for, seven Democrats against—in favor of Hayes.

Democrats threatened to boycott Hayes' inauguration. Rival governments arose claiming to recognize Tilden as the rightfully elected President. Republicans, fearing another sectional crisis, reached out to Democrats. In the Compromise of 1877 Democrats conceded the presidency to Hayes on the promise that all remaining troops would be removed from the South. In

March 1877, Hayes was inaugurated; in April, the remaining troops were ordered out of the South. The Compromise allowed southern Democrats to return to power, no longer fearing reprisal from federal troops or northern politicians for their flagrant violence and intimidation of black voters.

After 1877, Republicans no longer had the political capital to intervene in the South in cases of violence and electoral fraud. In certain locations with large populations of African Americans like South Carolina, freedpeople continued to hold some local offices for several years. Yet, with its most revolutionary aims thwarted by 1868, and economic depression and political turmoil taking even its most modest promises off the table by the early 1870s, most of the promises of Reconstruction were unmet. [2]

Conclusion

The end of Reconstruction, and the federal government's attempts to create a bi-racial democracy in the former Confederate states, ushered in a new era of white supremacy. After taking back control of state legislatures, conservative white Democrats created new state Constitutions that disfranchised black voters through arbitrary literary tests and burdensome poll taxes. Southern legislators also passed stringent new segregation or "Jim Crow" laws that rigidly segregated black and white passengers on trains and street cars and prohibited or limited African-American access to public places such as libraries, parks, hotels, and restaurants.

The federal government's failure to maintain the promises and ideals of Reconstruction meant that African-Americans would continue to fight for civil rights and equality throughout the late nineteenth and twentieth century. Only in the 1960s, during what some historians call the Second Reconstruction, would federal legislation finally strike down voter and segregation laws passed after the first Reconstruction that denied civil rights and equality under the law to African-Americans. [1]

11: Attributions

11.1: Footnote Attribution List

Module Attributions

(1) Content by Florida State College at Jacksonville is licensed under a CC BY 4.0

---

(2) The American Yawp is licensed under CC BY-SA 4.0 .

---

(3) Park Ethnography Program African American Heritage and Ethnography by the National Park Service is in the Public Domain .

---

(4) The American Revolution by the National Park Service is in the Public Domain .

---

(5) U.S. History by The Independence Hall Association is licensed under CC-BY 4.0

---

(6) *The Interesting Narrative of the Life of Olaudah Equiano, Or Gustavus Vassa, The African: Written By Himself* by Olaudah Equiano is in the Public Domain .

---

(7) A Journal of a Voyage Made in the Hannibal of London by Thomas Phillips is in the Public Domain .

---

(8) *Prayer* by John A. Lomax (Collector) has no known copyright restrictions.

---

(9) Go Preach My Gospel by John A. Lomax (Collector) has no know copyright restrictions.

---

(10) Jesus, My God, I Know His Name by John A. Lomax (Collector) has no know copyright restrictions.

---

(11) U.S. History by OpenStax is licensed under CC BY 4.0

---

(12) Boundless US History by Lumen Learning is licensed under CC-BY-SA 4.0

---

(13) David Walker, Walker's Appeal (Boston: David Walker, 1830) taken from http://docsouth.unc.edu/nc/walker/walker.html/en-en/menu.html is in the Public Domain .

---

(14) *A Memorial of William Lloyd Garrison from the City of Boston* by Boston (Mass.) City Council is in the Public Domain .

---

(15) "Felix" (Unknown) Slave Petition for Freedom (January 6. 1773) in *The Appendix: or Some observations on the expediency of the petition of the Africans living in Boston...* , by Lover of constitutional liberty is in the Public Domain .

---

(16) *Petition for freedom to the Massachusetts Council and the House of Representatives, January 1777* by Massachusetts Historical Societyis in the Public Domain .

---

(17) *Slow Drag Work Song* by John A. Lomax (Collector) has no known copyright restrictions.

---

(18) *Long Hot Summer Day* by John A. Lomax (Collector) has no known copyright restrictions.

---

(19) Sergeant A.M. Chandler of the 44th Mississippi Infantry Regiment, Co. F., and Silas Chandler, family slave, with Bowie knives, revolvers, pepper-box, shotgun, and canteen by Library of Congress is in the Public Domain .

---

(20) Letters from Spotswood Rice are in the Public Domain.

---

(21) *Letter to President Lincoln* by Hannah Johnson is in the Public Domain.

---

(22) *My Life in the South* by Jacob Stroyer is in the Public Domain.

---

(23) *Letter to the Editor of the Christian Recorder (May 10. 1864)* by George W. Hatton from the archives of Mother Bethel Church is in the Public Domain.

(24) Black Residents of Nashville to the Union Convention by Unknown persons in *Paying Freedom's Price: A History of African Americans in the Civil War* by Paul David Escott (pp 144-146) is in the Public Domain.

(25) *"I Hope to Fall With My Face to the Foe"* by Lewis Douglass is in the Public Domain .

(26) *Selections from the WPA interviews of formerly enslaved African Americans on Slavery* from the Works Progress Administration is in the Public Domain.

(27) *Maryland Slave to the President* by Annie Davis is in the Public Domain.

(28) *Selections from the WPA interviews of formerly enslaved African Americans on Being a Civil War Soldier* from the Works Progress Administration is in the Public Domain .

(29) *Thirty Years a Slave: From Bondage to Freedom* by Louis Hughes is in the Public Domain.

(30) *Selections from the WPA interviews of formerly enslaved African Americans on Emancipation* by the Works Progress Administration is in the Public Domain .

CC licensed content, Original

- Attributions. **Authored by**: Florida State College at Jacksonville. **License**: *CC BY: Attribution*

Index

D

dire